novum pocket

Ronald Brooks

The Reasons My Mum Suffered PTSD

novum ▲ pocket

© 2024 novum publishing

ISBN 978-3-903468-58-0
Cover photo and internal illustrations:
Ronald Brooks
Cover design, layout & typesetting:
novum publishing

The images provided by the author have been printed in the highest possible quality.

www.novum-publishing.co.uk

Print product with financial
climate contribution
ClimatePartner.com/16547-2311-1001

Contents

All the family are asleep in bed when suddenly:

Emmy (shrieking out loud): Where's Peter, where's Peter, where is my baby?

Fred (gently shaking her shoulder): Emmy love, wake up, wake up: you are having another nightmare.

Emmy: Where is Peter, have I left him on top of the bed again?

Fred: Emmy, wake up, please wake up: You are having another bad dream. Peter and Ron are both asleep in the small front bedroom, and Dot and Flo are asleep in the back bedroom. Everyone is alive and safe, believe me.

And then: It came to me like a bolt out the blue etc.

The Second World War followed on twenty years after the Great War, and in between there was the 'great depression'. These occurrences were calamitous for my mum and her family. It caused her mental and physical health problems.

When World War Two finished, mum was totally exhausted, had boils all over her body, and never totally recovered. Doctors put it down to her 'nerves' and effectively told her to 'get on with her life'. I think that was an unfair diagnosis.

Mum had my brother Peter on Easter Saturday 13 April 1941 in the middle of the Easter bombings, where the German bombers were trying to destroy Bristol City Docks, The Royal Edward Docks at Avonmouth, and The Bristol Aircraft Company (BAC) in Filton: the runway was less than two miles from our house. Four houses were demolished less than a quarter of a mile away. Our ceilings came down, our windows blown in, and the front door blown off its hinges.

Soldiers experiencing those type of situations are diagnosed with PTSD and it was many years later that I realised that women on the Home Front could suffer from it as well. I hope this poem will explain what I mean.

All my male relatives, other than my brother Peter (who missed out on doing National Service by 6 months) have served in the armed services. After each of the two wars they were lauded and deservedly given medals. Even I have a 'Veterans medal' for two years' National Service in North Devon.

Mum, on the other hand, was living in a war zone with four children to care for. We were bombed, very short of food, cold, hungry, and alone, and there were thousands of women looking after children in similar circumstances. And what did they get at the end of the wars? Zilch: nothing: little recognition, and no diagnosis of what they had suffered.

Germany needed a large area of land to achieve its ambition of becoming the world's greatest power and to feed its growing population. Hitler set about trying to conquer the world and establish an empire that would last for one thousand years: and he came very close to succeeding.

The British and Commonwealth people for two years stood alone, suffering a living nightmare: that should never, ever be forgotten.

It is too late for most of them now, but this is my attempt to show what they suffered. A government recognition would not go amiss as the last of those incredible women will soon pass away. Hopefully it may also encourage schools to enlighten children that this can happen here in the UK, as well as Ukraine.

I would also wish for children to be taught in detail what it is like to live through wars and poverty. At least now, Ukraine is showing what it is like to be invaded by an evil dictator.

All the family are asleep in bed when suddenly:

Emmy (shrieking out loud): 'Where's Peter, where's Peter, where is my baby'?

Fred (gently shaking her shoulder): 'Emmy love, wake up, wake up: you are having another nightmare.'

Emmy: 'Where is Peter, have I left him on top of the bed again?'

Fred: 'Emmy, wake up, please wake up: You are having another bad dream. Peter and Ron are both asleep in the small front bedroom, and Dot and Flo are asleep in the back bedroom. Everyone is alive and safe, believe me.'

And then: It came to me like a bolt out of the blue...

PTSD

It came to me like a bolt out of the blue
I suddenly realised that what I now knew
Rubbished conceptions of what doctors said
That mother had 'nerves' that had played
with her head

In fairness to doctors some things were obscure
Although you would have thought that after the war
Of 1914 when true horrors they saw
Research would have offered much more of a cure

Now they have realised that many had suffered
From nightmares and flashbacks and sweating
and trembling
Brought on by the horrors that they have endured
From accidents or assaults or trauma or war,
never ending

Post-Traumatic Stress Disorder is what they now call it
And treatment is now much more structured and wise.
But no one had thought long-gone events
could have caused it
And the true realisation brought tears to my eyes

P is for post meaning after and after
And after and after and after and after
An event that could give you so much distress
Your quality of life becomes an awful lot less

The event was the war and the period thereafter
When our cherished good life was reduced to disaster
Then the good times returned,
and the nightmares began
No one knew why: but I can now understand

T is for Trauma which started for sure
From the very beginning of the first great world war
Her father was conscripted and sent far away
No way to complain, no one had a say

History repeated itself twenty years later
When the same barbarians inflicted so much harm
Tried to destroy our dear nation and families
Took our dear father from us: what alarm

S is for stress that she suffered so badly
Four children to look after, all under eight
No food to feed them, no heat to warm them
And bombing to cope with, by day and by night

D is for Disorder, not the best of titles
Sounds as if you have eaten far too much trifle
Neither a disease, often no external symptoms
No one knew of it: all signs did she stifle

Mum's Early Years: If you can't say good about anybody, say nothing!

Her Mum and her Dad met when both
worked for a printers;
Allen Davies in Rupert Street,
close by where they both lived
Her Dad had lived on his own: his parents died early
And before long Gran realised,
she loved him most dearly

My Mum was born in nineteen 'o' nine
Her parents forced to get married:
the rules of that time
So, they immediately started off in squalid conditions
With a clash of religions and hopeless perdition

They lived in Bloomsbury Buildings,
off Charles Street, St. Paul's
A grim, cramped, rat-infested, dour city slum.
The only respite, the parks, and the downs
Where both parents tried to give
them a modicum of fun

The birth of mum's sister Florence Lilian Croome born 17 January 1913

Her sister Florence followed on 17 January, 1913
An added burden during times of conditions extreme
Poverty and homelessness, and trouble and strife
Not the best time to create, another young life

Mum started at St. James School
when she was just five
They had moved into number 3 Moon Street,
another right little dive
Just two rooms, but luckily it overlooked the school
Gran could watch them at play time,
so they didn't act the fool

And then the Great War started in 1914
And her Dad was conscripted, not wanted or foreseen
And off to India her Daddy was sent
Leaving her mum with yet another present!

The birth of mum's brother James William Croome (Uncle Bill) born 1 September 1915

The traumas increased when Mum was just five
With the birth of brother Bill, barely alive
Her Mum survived an horrendous conception
The pattern to come: Roman Catholic obsessions

Family helped by Grandad's uncle and aunt Jim and Fanny Trump and by Aunty Nell

Each little incident like the prick of a pin
The food just got scarcer; the people got thin
The cold weather chilled their bones to the core
And her nerves, totally frayed,
she could not take much more

Her Dad came home on compassionate leave
And made her Mum pregnant again, before he did leave
Birth control was a no-no for my Granny Croome
Even if for more children,
there was not that much room!

My Grandad was sent to the Western Front,
shortly thereafter
And there our troops met with total disaster
Many were captured; taken Prisoner of War
Their treatment was terrible, destroyed to the core

Then in that terrible conflict, her Daddy went missing
No one knew if he were dead or indeed alive
Under that dreadful mud of the battlefields
Prayers were said fervently for him to survive

Grandad captured by the Evil Huns

Then the Red Cross contacted my Grandma one day
To say that Grandad was far, far away
Captured by the Hun and confined in a cell
He was imprisoned there, brutally, for a very long spell

In great poverty, dire conditions
and very close to starving
The family survived on rotting fruit and stale bread
The Great War was raging, millions were dying
But at least her beloved Dad was alive, and not dead

Each little incident like the prick of a pin
The food just got scarcer; the people got thin
The cold weather chilled their bones to the core
Their nerves totally frayed;
they could not take much more

The birth of mum's sister Violet Croome (Aunty Vi) born 29 April 1917

And then came the birth of her dear sister Vi
Yet another addition said Granny Trump, with a sigh
How can we afford yet another hungry mouth?
With no news of daddy, their morale went south

Still, no one was sure if he was dead or alive
Had he been killed, or had he survived?
That obscene Great War was taking its toll
Even great grandma said, I cannot take much more

Food was a problem, never enough
Even if we had meat, it was always too tough
Bread and scrape, disgusting vegetables,
and thin watery soup
Not enough to fill us up to the roof

End of the Great War 1918

Up and down, good, and bad
One day happy, one day sad
Things got better and then things got worse
And before you know it, along comes the hearse

Mum's daddy gets repatriated: 1919

Her Daddy came back home in 1919
The skinniest man she had ever seen
Racked to his bones by ill health and famine
It was many years before he recovered his stamina

He met baby Violet for the very first time
And marvelled that all their children
were doing just fine
And it wasn't very long before he started a new life
And soon there was yet another baby, Arthur:
number five

And finally, he started to play football again
Hoping that in this sport he could find money and fame
For Bristol Clifton St. Vincent's on Bristol's lovely Downs
He was good and truly and deeply loved
this fine game

But even that joy turned soon to disaster
His leg badly broken, months spent in white plaster
His football career finished, life turned very grim,
A long time to recover, back on the dole yet again

And back to the bad days of poverty and grime
No social assistance was there at that time
The dreaded workhouse the only escape
But that was not an option: he could not lose face

Obnoxious Offal and Frugal Fodder from the Great War years

Emmy, please pop to the butcher's and see if you can
Get a scrag-end of mutton or a small neck of lamb
Be sure that you buy it in two separate sales
In that way you get, two turns of the scales

See if he has Chitterling, Pigs Trotters, or Pigs Cheek
Or a whole sheep's head, that would last us all week
Lamb's tongue, sheep's brains sheep's ears,
or sheep's nose
Whatever he is selling cheap, that's how it goes

But Mum, the food we are eating is disgusting and sad
Yesterday's slices of bull's heart, it made me quite bad
All stringy and tough and it tasted quite bitter
Although the liver and onions were a little bit better

When eating tough meat beware of the gristle
If it gets stuck in your throat be careful what you do
I remember Dad coughing and propelling it out
like a missile
And we siblings all ducked as past our heads it flew

I don't mind the kidneys with a little bit of steak
A little bit of cod or a little bit of hake
But those raw fish-eyeballs are really obscene
I watched Grandma suck one, and I wanted to scream!

And what about those cockles, whelks,
and gritty mussels
Why anyone would like them is really a puzzle
From Brian's Cockle shop in Bedminster:
you take your own basins
Then Grandma would eat them with great anticipation

Then there was Brawn made from pig's head
and trotters
Surrounded by jelly it really makes me squirm
Cow's heels, or jellied eels all sticky and wriggly
And winkles where with a pin, you pull out the worm

Tripe is the stomach of a cud-chewing ruminant,
Thick seam, thin seam or blanket it says on the sign
Eaten with a sprinkling of salt, pepper, and vinegar
After being cooked with onions in milk,
cream, or wine

Spam and ham, corned beef, and processed meats
Are a little bit nicer and more of a treat,
With pork bones you can make a very nice stew
Surprising what a little inspiration can do

Black pudding made just of bull's blood and guts
Stuffing made from apricots, herbs and nuts
And please don't feed me more sprouts or bread sauce
No ifs and no buts they really are coarse

Why can't we have nice food, like a good Sunday roast?
I am even quite partial to baked beans on toast
Faggots and peas from that Redcliffe Hill shop
Are really quite delicious and they don't cost a lot

Shepherd's Pie made from lamb or Cottage pie
made from beef
Each dish I love, and they are easy on the teeth
Stew with doughboys, but please not
the notorious Gruel
They feed that in workhouses and it is
incredibly cruel

Turnips and parsnips and nice roast potatoes
Bangers and mash with green mushy peas
Lettuce, spring onions and lovely red tomatoes
These are the nice foods so don't be a tease

And what about puddings all steaming and hot
Bread pudding should really not cost us a lot
Apple tart and custard, as long as it's not lumpy
Stewed rhubarb or rice pudding will stop
me being grumpy

Blackcurrants, gooseberries, blackberries, and plums
If we had a garden, we could grow with our chums
All make mouth-watering dishes, our lives to enhance
But in these slums of Bristol: not much of a chance!

But some puddings make me very forlorn
Sago and Tapioca puddings: they resemble frog spawn
If you make me eat them, I am certain to vomit
And then you will have to get me medicine or tonic

Then Grandma became wistful, her eyes sad and mist full.
I remember the Christmases before our lads went away
The roast chicken and potatoes with
stuffing and gravy
Those smells all come back to me in a nostalgic way

I am sorry my dearest, all these things are so true
But with virtually no money, are choices are few
So, close your eyes tight, and get it right down
Or you will turn into ugly if you keep up that frown

But I promise you one thing, Emmy my dear
They say this war will be over by this time next year
And your daddy will be back home with us again
And together we will help him get rid of his pain

We will have a brilliant party to celebrate, this mo-
mentous event
And all those terrible memories we will make
sure are spent
They say that this world war will hopefully end all wars
And Germany will never again darken our dear
English shores

We will put events behind us and get over this war
And have a great future, all safe and secure
And your bad dreams and nightmares will all go away
And so let us both plan for that wonderful day

First let's plan the menu, and so what would you like?
How about some sandwiches, some brown bread
and some white
Fish paste, meat paste, and egg from
Billy Button's chickens
With watercress grown on the windowsill
in our little kitchen

Lettuce sandwiches, beef sandwiches, tomato,
and cucumber
Coleman's mustard on ham that I boiled myself
Soaked in cold water to remove all traces of salt
Then boiled slowly for hours and left to cool
on the shelf

Egg mayonnaise, boiled eggs,
and home-made potato salad
Bread and dripping is lovely, I make it myself
The brown bit in the bottom, the tastiest treat
Spread it quite thickly on the bread and its ready to eat

Then we must have some sausage rolls,
all hot and all greasy
Made from sausage meat, with a raw egg mixed in
Wrapped and cooked in lovely puff pastry
Not to have these would be a terrible sin

Although it's not Christmas we must
have mince pies to eat
Made from dried fruit and spices;
strangely called mincemeat
With cinnamon, citrus zest and nutmeg
for extra flavouring
Then add a little splash of whisky,
alcoholic savouring!

Aunty Mary is a jam maker of home-made plum jam
She makes it each autumn, whenever she can
Gets fruit from the orchards all delicious and ripe
She never minds what fruit it is, whatever the type

For dessert we must have fresh strawberries and cream
Brought up from Cheddar in that little steam train
Tinned fruit salad, mandarin oranges, apricots,
peaches, or pears
Even evaporated milk will do, as nobody cares

A trifle made with jelly is an absolute must
With home-made custard and
whipped cream, we trust
On a bed of sponge fingers,
all soaked in Harvey's sherry
But please, not too much, or we will all end up merry!

Or we could make it from Bird's trifle
which comes in a packet
For those useless at cooking, you simply can't hack it
Little packets of ingredients with instruction to follow
And their dream topping is really
something to swallow

But a Knickerbocker Glory in a tall sundae glass
Sitting there eating it, we would feel
all elegant and sass
The dessert of my childhood dreams,
we could never afford
We would sit there in heaven,
dreaming we were abroad

To finish it off let's have some of
Grandad's great wine
Homemade from berries of all different kinds
Strawberries, blackberries, blackcurrants as well
His sloe gin and damson gin are really quite swell

And for the children real lemonade would be very nice
Made from fresh lemons, very thinly sliced
Steeped in boiling water, sugared, and then left to cool
No chance of them getting drunk and playing the fool!

And finally, two things to end the perfect party
Cheese and crackers with grapes, all very hearty
A little drop of port makes the cheese go down so nice
And then some Camp coffee, whatever the price

Outbreak of Spanish Flu: 1918

A dreadful outbreak of what became called Spanish Flu
Caused even more heartache and misery,
but what could we do?
Over five hundred million infected,
over fifty million died
More deaths from this epidemic than the Great War,
cannot be denied

It was spread by troops returning to
their native countries
The 18- to 30-year-olds were the ones
most badly infected
Their bodies were strong, but their
defence mechanisms lowered
Lungs filled with water, patient turned
blue and virtually drowned

Then, Bird Flu, the H1N1 Flu virus broke out
in the Etaples Army Camp
Close to Boulogne on the French Channel coast
Largest British Army reinforcement camp
ever established overseas
Another great problem to bring the world to its knees

Over three million personnel passed through
this camp in the war years
And millions of birds who carried
the pathogens headed our way
From the mouth of the river Somme
on their migration route
Nothing could stop them,
spreading horrendous infections, forsooth.

The birth of Mum's brother Arthur born 2 March 1923

Grandad seems to have rediscovered his strength!

Mum left school and went to work for Allen Davies's: rat in her coat pocket scared her to death: 1923

But then Mum's life was slowly getting better and better
A good job, good prospects and then came the icing.
She met my Dad, and they started courting
But at fifteen years old, her parents would not let her

A shock one day when leaving the factory
Her coat was stored in the basement dark, dirty, and grim
She put her hand in her pocket to get out her hanky
Out leapt a huge rat, her screams made a din!

In 1927 her spirits just soared
Again, she started to see my dad, the boy she adored
Would he still love her, could he still love her?
But still she was worried about what her parents might say

They rekindled their friendship, that heart-warming day
He was determined to woo her, there was no other way
So, he started to pursue her, she felt so gay
And they didn't give a hoot what her parents might say

I wonder what he will buy me for Christmas, Mum pondered
She knew that around the shops he had wandered
But oh, what a wonderful shock it would be
When on Christmas Eve 1929 he proposed:
down on one knee.

And so, on 20 July 1931 at St. Peter's Registry they wed
But Granny Brooks was not happy with her son Fred
Neither was Granny Croome with Emmy,
for the very same reason
Both major wage earners were leaving home
and that was real treason!

They married and on their wedding day,
left to live in the Brum
But no parents applauded them or joined in their fun
They started their own business, a nice little bike shop
Both worked most hard and aimed for the top.

At first the business just prospered and prospered
They built up the business which people respected
Moved to a new flat, much better and larger
What was to come, they could not have expected

A person purporting to be their very best friend
Swindled the business and brought it to an end
To Bristol they returned to rebuild their shattered lives
And to start our young family, and for us to provide

Arthur gets scalded and terrible poverty

From laughter to tears, Uncle Arthur was scalded
A pot full of hot tea spilt accidentally, all down his back
Up and down, good, and bad
Happy as Larry, then terribly sad

Arthur was scarred for the rest of his life
Much more trouble, and much more strife
With no NHS to look after and care for him
Life really was, terribly, horribly grim.

What a dreadful beginning to Mum's early life!
A world full of poverty, anguish, and strife
War, food shortages, privations and more
It is a wonder that she was not bitter to the core

Then came that cruel American Wall Street crash
Which sent around the world a terrible blast,
Jobless and wage less the bad times returned
Would there ever be a consistent time
when money was earned?

Each little incident like the prick of a pin
The food just got scarcer; the people got thin
The cold weather chilled their bones to the core
And her nerves, totally frayed,
she could not take much more

Up and down, happy, and sad
One minute good and then one minute bad
Rarely stable, rarely cool
Play the clown or play the fool.

The birth of mum's brother Stanley Ronald born 12 May 1927

In between all this trauma, her fifth sibling was born
Although no further children her Mother had sworn
A brother named Stanley Ronald came into their life
Causing yet more hardship, trouble and strife

A great toll on her mother who was confined to her bed
I will look after your children, her sister Nell said
Stop your shenanigans: no more children you need
If you carry on like this, you will end up deceased

Then Grandad relented and said Stanley could be
Brought up Roman Catholic, so he then could see,
A different religion, but this did not work
Stanley rebelled against it, and caused further hurt

Mum always said she had a good childhood
Lots of love, picnics, sister and brotherhood
Although money was scarce and eight mouths to feed
Good cooking and love satisfied all of their needs

Broadmead Baptist Church brought them very great solace
Friendships and faith a very great comfort
And right up until the very end of her life
Mum used her faith to battle hardship and strife

Things got better; things got worse
Sometimes they had money in their purse
Sometimes food was upon the table
But they all survived the best they were able

And then came the episode most difficult to mention
It filled the household with division and tension
It gave my Aunty Vi a whole lot of flak
Oh! horror of horrors her boyfriend was black

In those days mixed marriages
were a dreadful disgrace
To your neighbours and friends',
you could not show your face
The family was split, its harmony was lost
But Violet was determined whether they liked it or not

If you accept your boyfriend, you must leave this house
Saying nothing Vi walked out, as meek as a mouse
My Mother was mortified, her best friend was gone
My Grandmother was adamant that she
had done nothing wrong

Aunty Vi went to live in a ramshackle apartment
In St. Pauls, where many were poor
and seriously deprived
My Mum would secretly visit her
and helped her survive
If Grandma had found out,
mum would have been eaten alive!

The Good Years: 1934–1938

The period from 1934 to 1938 turned into very good years:
A new house, two lovely daughters and a husband so dear
A good job and prospects, and food in abundance
Money to spend, joy to be had and little to fear

Dad set about building a caravan from nothing
To tow to the Brean Sands, near the Weston resort
A holiday for us was his honest intentions
He was a very accomplished tradesman,
I'm pleased to report

It got even better when in November of 1938,
On the fourteenth of the month, I appeared on the scene
Like my siblings I should have been born on the thirteenth
But, unlike me, I arrived just five minutes late!

I was the baby boy, that they had both prayed and craved for
Adored by my sisters and loved by them both
For a while we all lived totally charmed lives
But the dark clouds were gathering,
heed the warnings forsooth

And then I fell ill and was in a great deal of trouble
My mum told me I was rushed to the children's hospital
In a bus driven rapidly by my dear Uncle Bill
I was really in trouble: extremely sickly and very, very ill

My parents were not allowed in the ward to see me
They could only just look at me through the ward door
A milk infection they said, had seriously affected me
They did not know if I would survive as there
was no known cure

I survived, but I was a very fragile little baby
Underweight and prone to most of the ills
But Mum worked her wonders and slowly revived me
But the trauma had left her stressed out to the gills

Then slowly the fear of war started building
The monsters were gathering, in secret abroad
And memories were slowly resurfacing, and worrying
Of the horrors and death of that dreadful great war

With Hitler and his cronies now in the ascendance
Quietly pursuing their disgusting and evil intents
Their strength they were building,
their enemies blindsiding
And all those in power just looked the other way

For all you in power just remember this ode
There is no recompense for a cowardly code
For if you are someone who just looks away
Your come-uppance will follow you for many a day

The horrors and suffering and death of that war
The memories flooded back from each, a little bit more
Information that said the fiends are now moving
With evil intent: their grand plan to proving

Each little incident like the prick of a pin
The food just got scarcer; the people got thin
The cold weather chilled your bones to the core
And her nerves, totally frayed,
she could not take much more

The Second World War Years

Prelude to war: The Nazis hatred of the Jewish People
October 28, 1938

Hitler and Mussolini, the Nazis and Fascists
Were determined to rule the modern-day world
By hook or by crook they would dominate all kingdoms
Deprive us of our freedoms and put many to the sword

Most Germans were bitter by their past privations
Imposed when they lost that first great war
But that was their come-uppance
for the hardships delivered
To hordes of decent people right through to the core

Germany expelled Polish Jews from all its territories
About 17,000 Polish Jews to Poland were forced
But Poland refused to allow the Jews entrance
And most were stranded,
abandoned in the no-man's-land

The Night of the Broken Glass
(Kristallnacht): 9 November 1938

In an act of despair over the fate of his parents
A diplomat in Paris was shot by a young Jewish man
The Nazis use this act to enhance antisemitic harassment,
The Night known known as Kristallnacht
or Broken Glass began

Several dozen Jews lost their lives in this terrible fracas
Tens of thousands of Jews to concentration
camps were sent
Storm Troopers destroyed their homes and their businesses
Not even their houses of worship, did they relent

The suffering of Jewish children in German
and Austria was appalling
Allowed to enter museums, public playgrounds,
and swimming pools they were not
Expelled from public schools, ostracised, and abused
By which many Arian Germans were very highly amused

Segregated and ostracised and in total despair,
Many Jewish adults committed suicide
from desperation and fear
Most families tried desperately their homeland to leave
By land, or by air and even by sea

The Government agreed that in these desperate times
Unaccompanied Jewish children would be welcome,
here to reside
Promises were made that homes for all refugees
they would find
And on BBC radio and around the Country
appeals were made

On 2 December 1938 at the Port of Harwich
The first party of nearly 200 Kindertransport children arrived
Leaving their parents, siblings and relatives behind
Safe at last from their freedoms, by Hitler denied

Almost 10,000 unaccompanied, mainly Jewish,
children followed in sequence
Confirming the information that was now being heard
What, my Mother said, would they do to our children?
If this is what they can do to their own dependants

More ominous rumours and dark clouds from Europe
Where Germany was girding its loins to recover
Its lands and possessions they considered their right
Stolen by the signing of the Treaty of Versailles

Hitler decided the Great War had not finished
In that humiliating surrender, in that railway carriage in 1918
It was put on hold until their new plans succeeded
And the third Reich would rise up and dominate again

The Germans were bitter at their privations
Following the Treaty of Versailles in 1918
Their lands had been split up;
their powers decreased
And inflation meant money had no virtual worth

Their women had been violently raped by the Russians
In response for the violations done to their own
And Russian cities had been reduced to rubble
And few Germans cared they had caused all this trouble

Their economy in tatters, inflation out of control
A barrow full of money was worth little more
No money to buy any food or resources
They were seething with injustice right through
to the core

The desire was for a new Reich that would
last a millennium
And show the world how to live and be proud
But only for those of Aryan descendant
Others were doomed to be dust in the ground

The Jews were the first people doomed to suffer
with no grace
With obscene anti-Semitic laws and oppression
In Germany and Italy, the world watched the disgrace
Of an attempt to wipe out, a whole Jewish race

First the publication in 1938 called The Manifesto of Race,
Was a creed to wipe Jewish people from this earth's face
Then through the Racial Laws in Fascist Italy
Ever increasingly the Jews were treated pitifully

The entire world was exhausted by the war
recently finished,
At just over two short decades years ago
And was willing to do almost anything
to avoid further conflict
And the message to the politicians was very explicit

It has been said many times that all it needs to happen
Is for good men to do nothing, for evil to succeed
So, turning a blind eye to satisfy the current need
Gave Hitler the freedom to do as he pleased

No reaction was made to the annexation of Austria
in March 1938
Nor to the Sudeten area of Czechoslovakia
later in September
Many people were escaping the grasps
of those heathens
And the tales being told were a total disgrace
to remember

Hitler, Franco, and Mussolini and their Fascist dream
Had slowly been building up manpower, weapons:
an awesome team
The Russians were willing to stand by and watch
A cut of the spoils was their hope they could snatch

In Italy anti-Semitic laws stripped the Jews
of their citizenship
And governmental and professional work of any kind
Adolf Hitler had enormous influence over Benito Mussolini
Since Italy had become allied with Nazi Germany

Germany started to round up the Jews and herded
them into Ghettoes
Where there was nowhere to escape or to hide
Then they were sent to appalling concentration camps
Where Hitler had one 'single aim: – genocide'.

Franco's success for the world was a disaster
It encouraged Hitler to make his first move
In February 1938 a Nazi plot was uncovered
With German speaking Austrian Nazis wanting
to join the Nazi masters

A referendum was called for the Austrian people
To see if there was any support for the move
But before it could be carried out in a democratic fashion
Germany invaded and 'assumed' Austria,
the people had no say

On 1 September 1939 Hitler began the Polish invasion
1,300 planes of his Luftwaffe (German air force) he sent
2,000 tanks and 1.5 million ground troopers
On complete annihilation, he was hell bent.

Hitler looked for his next tactical Polish Target
The Port of Danzig, his infamous choice
Of huge strategic importance to Germany's progress
That was the next place to suffer much strife

France and the UK issued their final ultimatum
Stop what you are doing: we can take no more
Hitler ignored this, and World War Two was unavoidable
As if Hitler would contemplate withdrawal:
he was his own law

Germany and Russia's defeat of Poland was swift
and ruthless
Within two days the Polish air force had been
completely obliterated
Poland was divided between those two rogue nations
Now the world really had to decide just what it would do

Mum and Dad's hopes and dreams were evaporating rapidly
With each little incident being like the prick of a pin
The odds of avoiding war just got shorter and shorter,
And Mum's nerves, totally frayed, had got very thin

As Germany began ramping up its intentions for war
The Soviets agreed that in exchange for some land
Not to attack Germany, they let them proceed
Our forces, we were virtually useless, unable to take a
positive stand

Appeasement by British Prime Minster Neville Chamberlain: 1939

We were economically, militarily, and politically depleted
British Prime Minster Neville Chamberlain,
a total pip squeak
Obsequious, a weakling, an appeaser of the worst kind
He was hopelessly inadequate to deal with these fiends

What worries me now is that in many respects
Chamberlain and Jeremy Corbyn share many defects
A pacifist with ideas dangerous to freedom and democracy
And the great many threats we face in a world
challenged by autocracy

The filmmakers captured Chamberlain returning
to England,
Symbolically waving a piece of white paper
Declaring that he had secured 'peace in our time'.
By allowing Germany to 'assume' Sudetenland,
by him that was fine'

Confident these appeasements had averted a total war
For a brief time, the anxieties of people were allayed
Mum and dad breathed a sigh of relief for a moment
But the rat in the grass would not go away.

Trust in Hitler was badly misplaced by our leaders,
He was lying and cheating the whole of the time
He was a bully who relied on such gentle appeasers,
Eager to get peace whatever the price

Our own Royal family came under a cloud
Grave cause for security was voiced right out loud
As the King who had abdicated, for the sake of his wife
Praised Hitler out loud, which caused us great strife

Weak Czechoslovakia was Hitler's very next gambit
Divided into two countries in 1919 (Czechoslovakia
and Slovakia)
Many Germans felt isolated and totally abandoned
A dangerously ticking bomb was festering away

Germany and Russia made a 'non-aggression' pact
To reverse the existing position and to put things right back
Divide up Czechoslovakia, Germany seized
Slovakia as it may,
Yet again only weak opposition from France and the UK.

Child Evacuation 1939

Memories of the Zeppelin, raids of the Great War
When thousands of children died, and there was more
Thousands were injured and suffered for life
A great many years of suffering and strife

Plans were made to evacuate all children,
even before the declaration of war
And within four days of its declaration,
Operation Pied Piper was actioned
A million children and their teachers
on to trains were loaded
To be transported to safety,
though some had to be goaded!

More than three million British children
were displaced from their homes
To distant Canada, Australia, the USA,
away from their Mums
Some, to the British countryside and villages were sent
And for young and for all, it was a heart stopping wrench

Then came for Mum a life changing decision
To keep us kids with her, or to send us away
To safer locations, far out in the country
A decision that filled her with total dismay

My brother-in-law Dennis and his young brother Ivor
Were evacuated to St. Dennis in Cornwall in haste
They were billeted with people who did not
really want them
Their horror of being away from home
had begun with distaste

They had a totally miserable existence, badly mistreat-
ed and seriously starved
Looked after by people who had no morals at all
Beating them, abusing them, starving,
and cheating them
Slave labour today is what it is called

Some evacuees were treated royally by their new hosts
Who loved them, revered them,
and later missed them the most
Some stayed in contact for the rest of their lives
But sadly, this was more the exception than the rule

Mum decided to keep all of us together
All under one roof was her final call
At home in Southmead where she could look after us all
Even as the bombs and incendiaries, started to fall

This heart-breaking decision was hard to decide
And some who did not understand, would later deride
How could you have put, your dear children at risk
Or were you not putting your selfish person first?

Mum made her decision on a well thought out premise
That if anyone was going to die, they would not die alone
No matter how bad things could get,
and this looked so likely
We would all die together, all loved and at home

Now, let me introduce my good friend Edward (Ted) Hall
We met at the gates of the local infants school
We have had a friendship for seventy-five years
Through good times and bad times, happiness, and tears

The Government had a policy of splitting up brothers
At the height of the war, so no family would suffer
The trauma of having multiple male sibling deaths
As happened before, with devastating effects

So, his brother Norman was sent away to the country
To live with his gran and grandfather all on his own
Travel was difficult, controlled by the government
And not even the chance of a chat on the phone

Ted's dad was the publican, a Protected Occupation
At the 'Welcome Inn' in Southmead, a wonderful pub
Providing relaxation, recreation, and some normal living
But risking his life as Fire and Air Raid Warden was
the other side of the rub

Which meant that the siblings were for years far apart
To think of that sadness, puts a tear in my heart
Each effectively grew up as the only child
Lonely and longing to play together in the wild

Oh, the struggle, oh the pain
When will my beloved husband be home again?
To help me take these dreadful decisions
That some people looked upon with selfish derision.

Declaration of War 1939

Great Britain and France, honoured their treaty with Poland,
And on September the third declared war on the foe
But resources were low and the response very poor
And Poland was quickly taken out of the war

The Polish military were no match for
this unstoppable force
Foot soldiers, old weapons, lances, and horse
The odds were stacked against them, all totally antiquate
Their defence was strong but inadequate, it sealed their fate

Many from Poland escaped to the West
Where together they did their very best
To defeat the ogres who had taken away
Their freedom, their homeland, their relatives,
all put to the test

Hitler on the other hand, had entirely different plans
His complete domination of the world, we now understand
He completely disregarded the Treaty of Versailles
And the Nazi-Soviet Non-aggression Pact: just tossed aside

The Second World War, was a global disaster
That lasted six long and exhausting years
Every day was a difficult one,
every day was a dangerous one
And not a single day went passed without
somewhere death, tears, and fears

At 11:30p.m on 2 September, Chamberlain's Cabinet
met for one final meeting
A thunderstorm outside emphasised the darkness,
our plight, and the gloom
The ultimatum would be presented in Berlin
at nine o'clock next morning
To expire at eleven o'clock,
before the House of Commons convened at noon.

At 11:15 next morning the third of September 1939
The nation held its breath hoping all would be fine
Chamberlain addressed the nation by radio, and told the world:

'This morning, the British ambassador in Berlin, handed to the German Government, a final note, stating emphatically that unless we hear from you, by 11 o'clock, that you are prepared, at once, to withdraw your troops from Poland, a state of war will exist between us.

I must tell you that no such undertaking has been received, and that consequently, this country is now at war with Germany. We have a clear conscience; we have done all that any country could do to establish peace. The situation in which no word given by Germany's ruler could be trusted, and no people or country could feel itself safe has become intolerable.

Now may God bless you all. May he defend the right. It is the evil things we shall be fighting against – brute force, bad faith, injustice, oppression, and persecution – and against them I am certain that the right will prevail.'

Chamberlain addressed the House of Commons at its first Sunday session in over 120 years. He spoke to a quiet House in a statement which even opponents termed 'restrained and therefore effective:

'Everything that I have worked for, everything that I have hoped for, everything that I have believed in during my public life has crashed into ruins. There is only one thing left for me to do: that is to devote what strength and power I have, forwarding the victory of the cause for which we have sacrificed so much'.

Mum and dad were totally devastated,
they knew what was to come
Death, destruction, and every hardship,
everywhere under the sun
Those terrors of the Great War against
Germany flooding back in spades
How many would survive by the end of the decade?

The Phoney War

From October 1939 to March, mystifyingly,
no hostilities occurred
No land operations undertaken by the Allies or
Germans took place
Both sides were building up their diminished reserves
Neither side wanting to fail or to start losing face

People began to get extremely complacent
This wasn't so bad as they thought after all
Our men will be back from the front in an instant
And those Nazi fiends we will be able to stall

And then out of the blue a state of total war hit us
The horror and carnage was way beyond belief
More than 100 million people from over 30 countries
And for six long years there would be no relief

In every garden an air raid shelter was built
Anderson or Morrison it really mattered naught
It made everyone totally aware of how serious things were
Of the dangers we faced: our fears started
to make us rigid and fraught

We then heard sounds of the sirens start wailing
Bringing disaster out of sky to many a house
And when the German bombers started their blitzkrieg
We kids had to be as quiet as a mouse

King George V1 gave a radio broadcast,
addressing the nation
Mum described it to me as a devastating affair
She could remember the privations of the
First Great World War
When in that prisoner of war camp,
her beloved dad was left in total fear

War and the invaders get closer: 1940

March 1940 and the Russians invaded Finland again
They defeated their army, causing so much hurt,
death and pain
Denmark and Norway were then overwhelmed by the foe
And to France and to England the fiends planned to go

Dutch farmworkers sympathetic to Hitler,
ahead of the planned invasion appeared
To start cutting out secret landing strips
for the Nazi aircraft we feared
Fortunately, these were spotted by
the Royal Air Force in flight
Destroyed them and the perpetrators
disappeared into the night

The French depended on the Maginot Line for their defence
And heavily reinforced it: that seemed to make sense
But German troops went above it and
through the Arden Forest,
Virtually impossible to do, the experts had promised!

Germany had superiority in the air by now
And so, the war expanded so quickly and how,
On 14 March 1940 into Paris, they marched
And Parisiennes could only look on in total dismay,
a stab in the heart.

There is the famous (or infamous) photograph
of horrible Hitler
Surveying and gloating in front of the glorious Eiffel Tower,
Laughing with glee at what had now become his realm
For a millennium, he swore, Germans would
now take the helm

France surrendered to the Nazis:
22 June 1940

Then Calais and Boulogne were
overrun by the brutes
And our troops were ordered
to reach Dunkirk if they could
A large-scale evacuation was being
planned back at home
Stay on the beaches and we will get
boats to your zone.

Fortunately for our troops Hitler decided
to halt the Panzer advance
To allow his infantry to catch up, he reckoned
escape for the British: no chance
But this gave our troops an additional,
invaluable, couple of days.
And then the weather changed helping us
in a great many ways

Operation Dynamo

Operation Dynamo was put in place
and the evacuation commenced
Every boat over 30 feet long with a shallow
draft must assist, no sitting on the fence
The response was amazing, and the RAF
kept the Luftwaffe away from the beaches
The French Army held their positions under
very fierce attack: a miracle completed

Altogether 338, 226 Allied soldiers were evacuated between
27 May and 4 June 1940.

Operation Ariel

Operation Ariel followed, 15 to the 25 June:
Some 30,360 men were rescued from Cherbourg,
21,474 from St. Malo, Over 50,000 from Brest,
St. Nazaire, and La Pallice.

During Operation Ariel, the official number of Allied soldiers and airmen rescued amounted to 191, 870 of whom 144, 171 were British; all to fight another day.

Bristol Blitz: 1940s

Black-out was enforced and the city advertising
lights shut down
Thick curtains the rule, not a glimpse of light to be shown
Air Raid Wardens patrolled the streets:
'PUT OUT THAT LIGHT.'
Even car headlights were 'hooded',
you would not want to drive at night

The very first air raid on the Bristol Aircraft Company
at Filton
Was on 19 June 1940: the start of the many
It was an attack by a single bomber,
a recognisance manoeuvre
Not much damage was done,
and it was very quickly all over.

My father recalled how one evening he went
Up on Filton Golf Links to observe an event
Fighters in combat, weaving and wheeling
Silhouetted against a brilliant blue ceiling

Our pilots were desperate to protect our dear land
From the hordes of bombers approaching in bands
There were hundreds of bombers with one evil intent
To destroy us completely, on this they were hell bent

Then shortly afterwards there was a major air raid
No warning was given, everyone was afraid
Mum was talking to Mrs Marshall, our neighbour next door,
When they saw this great mass of aircraft,
they dived to the floor.

They quickly recovered and ran into the house
She put me under the table, please be as quiet as a
mouse, she said.
Both Dot and Flo were at school, away at that time
Mum was petrified: had they survived and were they
both fine?

After the raid Mum took me in the pram
To meet Flo from school, the Doncaster Road one
And then on to Fonthill Road School to collect
our sister Dot
Already she was on her way home with Joan Smith:
they were not worried a jot!

My memory is clear of one particular night's bombing
raid that year
When Mum was alone, afraid and in great fear
When the warning sirens sounded, to alleviate her fears
We decamped to the Smith house, all in floods of tears

There was Kenny and Wally, Mervyn, and Joan
Their mum Edie Smith and my Mum were there too
Our little family made up the numbers that day
Dorothy, Florence, and me: and Peter
was imminently due!

Whilst worrying for us and not making a fuss
Mum was worried for her relatives overseas
In foreign countries, some near and some far
Mum prayed for them down on her knees

In the front room all seven children were laid down to relax
As close to the dividing wall as well as we could
Away from the front window with the X covered glass
You are very safe now, said Mum, so please be very good.

We could hear the loud crashes and see the light flashes
The ground shook below us as the bombs rained down
It went on for hours, no sleep could we manage
We just prayed we would be safe until morning
came around.

Uncle George was a Fireman in grave danger at Filton
One of Mum's favourite brothers-in-law
Putting out fires as the Nazis bombed hell out of us
It is hard to imagine the images he saw.

Worrying whether he had survived the raid
Wondering how many people that day he had saved
Hoping he had lived through yet another hard night
Worrying, worrying, worrying, and worrying:
would there ever be an end in sight?

The danger had started, the nightmare had begun
We could all say goodbye to the good times and fun
No more trips to the seaside, no more picnics
on the Downs,
The military had moved in, and these were
all out of bounds

Overnight of the 6/7 December 1940 Bristol's
famous old city centre
Was blitzed, causing immense damage,
injury, and death
That night, my Granny Brooks' brother,
Shadrach Rowe, was killed in the onslaught
He was 63 years old with a family,
and everyone was totally bereft

Wartime Food Rationing: 8 January 1940

People were put on a very strict war footing
Gas masks were issued, and blackout enforced,
Brown paper strips put in a cross in each window
And identity cards to be carried by all

Areas of land were cut off from the nation
Some farmers were deprived of their land and their homes
Barbed wire was placed at a great many locations
To protect us from the invasion of those precious zones.

Rationing was introduced for one and for all
This did not stop some thieves and
some rich people, how cruel
Squirrelling many items of food and
wine commodities away
Black-marketeers and spivs the order of the day

From the very beginning of war, severe austerity started
With the beginning of food rationing, the future was bleak
Each adult was allowed a mere 4oz of bacon,
2oz of butter and a measly half pound of sugar per week

Meat, tea, jam, cheese, eggs, and milk were soon added
To the list of rationed products and goods
Imported fruits such as lemons, bananas,
and other fruit crops
All virtually disappeared from the shelves of shops

The Ministry of Food controlled every aspect of our diet
And produced many leaflets to help, advise and educate.
Books such as 'What's left in the Larder' by Ambrose Heath
Making use of all leftovers, although not good for our teeth

Each little incident like the prick of a pin
The food just got shorter; the people got thin
The cold weather chilled your bones to the core
And her nerves, totally frayed, she could not take
much more

We queue for our bread, and we queue for our meat
In the cold, in the rain or even the heat
Standing outside of shops for hours in
the stark crowded streets
Whatever you have, storekeeper,
we will be happy to eat

Pig bins were attached to every lamp post,
in every street
In which you must put any food you could not eat
Left-over food! Hmmm, there wasn't much
chance of that,
In our house we eat every single food scrap

Leave home by 6.00a.m. whatever the weather
Walk to the shops and join the long queues
What will we get today from the Co-op store?
A little bit less or a little bit more?

Cold weather, hot weather, sunshine, or rain
We stood there together all sharing the pain
The anxiety of whether the food would arrive
So that for yet another day we could survive

Gossips and rumours what's false and what's true?
Everything is a worry, but what can you do?
Children to care for, chores to be done
Your husband away in the hot desert sun

Make do and mend was the theme of those days
Nothing was wasted, everything saved
Wool was recycled, saucepans repaired
You must be savvy when there is nothing, so there!

We stood there for hours; the Mums liked to natter
But often so cold our teeth started to chatter
I clasped Mum's hand very tightly indeed,
Even as a child I recognised our need

Our feet were so cold, our toes were in pain
We stamped our feet, but it was all in vain
Our shoes were worn out, the bottoms in holes
With thin cardboard inside, to beef up the soles

The milkman came down the path, and he did not tarry
His silver gleaming milk churn he struggled to carry
Mum watched him carefully as he ladled out full measures
The white creamy milk was a veritable treasure
Milk for breakfast, milk in tea
Bread and hot milk were so often our feed
No fancy cereals, no reasons to diet
But bread and sugar: we loved it, why don't you try it!

Children were taught to be extremely obedient
If the Germans invade, we would all need to hide
Senseless chatter or noise would reveal us
The outcome would create unpleasantness and fuss

Belgium and Holland invaded and fall in just 10 days: April 1940

Churchill became Prime Minister and took charge
on the tenth of May,
Controlling the war cabinet, he would now have his say
Along with Clem Atlee the coalition went well
Together they eventually saved of us,
from the very jaws of hell

That very day was dreadful, with huge
and widespread destruction
As Hitler launched his Blitzkrieg on the ill-prepared world
His troops then drove forward into Belgium and Holland
Sweeping all before them and putting many to the sword

The German Panzer divisions broke through the Ardennes
And spread quickly throughout the green fields of France
With the French troops stranded in the Maginot Line
The allies, though brave, did not have a chance

The Germans advanced through France like a whirlwind
The Allies ruthlessly overrun, at a terrifyingly fast pace
Retreating troops were hampered: thousands
of refugees were fleeing
The West facing defeat, humiliation,
and to seriously lose face

German progress continued at a very fast pace
Fleeing refugees hampered the retreating troops,
total fear on their faces
Their goods piled high, but where on earth could they go?
What would happen to them, they really didn't know

The Huns they are coming, just a few miles away
They could be on our beaches, later today
Come children quickly, get your gas masks put on
Do exactly as I tell you, please do nothing wrong

I know that I sent that horrible man away
When he came with your gas masks, the other day
But what he told us now makes very good sense
People dying from gassing will not help our defence

Mustard gas is a despicable weapon
Used by the Huns on the brutal Great Western Front
Despite worldwide condemnation their plan is so clear
To defeat us, the last standing enemy,
the one that they fear

Everyone must be at their most aggressive peak
To defeat the Huns when they land on the beach
To fail at the first hurdle would be a disgrace
We must stand, we must fight,
we must defend every space

Churchill's War Speeches: 13 May 1940

Winston Churchill, as Prime Minister,
at his first address said:
"*I have nothing to offer but blood, toil, tears and sweat.*
We will defeat these barbarians, come what may,
Until the war is over, I am here to stay."

Things got worse by the twentieth of May
The Germans had reached Amiens
and the coast by next day
Splitting the British troops into two separate groups
Now we were really in the soup

Each little incident like the prick of a pin
The food just got scarcer; the people got thin
The cold weather chilled your bones to the core
And Mum's nerves, totally frayed,
she could not take much more

Dunkirk: Operation Sea Lion: 27 May 1940

The night before the rescue plan was put into place
King George the sixth made a plea to our race
Please pray for our troops to return to us safely
They need all the spiritual help that we can
possibly summon

Trapped on the beaches with nowhere to go
Strafed by the fighters, bombed by the foe
A miracle happened and most got away
And thank goodness they were able to fight another day

Constantly harassed by fighters and bombers
Trying to kill all those brave men on the beaches
The screaming, the whistling of diving Stukkah fighters
Strafing to wipe the lives of our helpless lads away

Men turned to jelly, a terrible fear in the belly,
Helping each other the best that they could
Waiting for rescue, with no hope of water or food
Helping injured comrades to help raise the mood

Around 700 little ships set sail from ports
To cross the channel with larger escorts
From north, south, east, and west, they all hove
To rescue our soldiers and bring them back home

Motor launches, lifeboats, barges, and even private yachts
All took their part in this daring-deed plot
Paddle steamers, the Mersey Ferry, Barges as well
Even a fifteen-foot fishing boat (Tamzine) battled the swell

The paddle steamer the Medway Queen
One of the bravest little boats ever seen
Did a total of seven round trips through that hostile place
And rescued 7,000 men, through God's amazing grace

A miracle happened and most got away
And thank goodness they were there to fight another day
The Dunkirk sprit was what it was called
And whilst many were killed, many more were restored

Those that were captured were treated horrendously
The Geneva Convention of 1929 was completely ignored
Prisoners were shot as soon as they were captured
Of humane convention: Germans did not give a jot.

The Geneva Convention of 27 July, 1929
Laid down the treatment of prisoners of war for all time
Captives must always be treated humanely and protected
From violence, insults, public curiosity
and reprisals against them

But rumours quickly surfaced of the Nazi atrocities
On the very day, men of the Royal Norfolk Regiment surrendered
Having run out of ammunition in the village of Paradis
All shot in cold blood by the animals of the SS.

Our boys came back from the front badly beaten
Ragged, exhausted, and shaking with fear
Could we ever gain victory from the jaws of defeat?
That would take a great many years

To see those men, return from the trenches
Skin burnt, eyes blinded, fear on their faces
Hand on the shoulder of the man just in front
The League of Nations seemed as weak as a runt

Mustard gas was a despicable weapon
Used by the Hun on that savage Western Front
Despite worldwide condemnation their plan was so clear
To defeat us, the last standing enemy,
the one they most feared

But there was one concession Mum was
not prepared to accede
Putting baby Peter in a respirator, she totally disagreed
Instead, a cover of gauze placed lovingly over his head
Would surely protect him from ending up dead.

Each little incident like the prick of a pin
The food just got shorter; the people got thin
The thought of being gassed, chilled your bones to the core
And her nerves, totally frayed, she could not
take much more

As it turned out, Hitler never had a chance
Our brave fighter pilots gave him a kick up the pants
The invasion was aborted, the danger had passed
Her little family brood was much safer at last.

But the bombing continued, the devastation immense
Many houses destroyed that was Hitler's intent
But Mum still managed to hold her sanity intact
And provide life for our family: that is a fact.

On 4 June 1940 Churchill made this famous speech

To put it in rhyme would be most indiscreet.
His words to the House of Commons
were poetry of the elite
Rousing and full of most eloquent stuff
And nobody thought he was trying to bluff.

He said:
"We shall defend our Island, whatever the cost may be.
We shall fight on the beaches, we shall fight on the landing grounds,
We shall fight in the fields and in the streets,
we shall fight in the hills.
We shall never surrender"

The Sinking of the RMS Lancastria
17 June 1940 while evacuating troops
from St. Nazaire

RMS Lancastria was a British ocean liner
Requisitioned by the UK Government at the start of the war
It was sunk with the largest loss of life
from a single conflict engagement
A war crime, an act of barbarianism: total enragement

On 17 June 1940 one of the worst maritime
disasters ever took place
Close to the French Port of Saint-Nazaire,
in peacetime, a beautiful place
About 4,000 men, women and children died
in the disaster there
Sunk by German planes, fewer than 2,500 survived:
what total despair

She was used on Operation Aerial,
shortly after the Dunkirk evacuation,
An emergency order to evacuate British
civilians and troops from the ports of France
With a legal capacity of 1,300 passengers,
they were squashed in like sardines
Yet another disaster hushed up to protect morale,
so it would seem

On 18 June 1940 Churchill told
the House of Commons:

'Let us therefore brace ourselves to our duties,
And so, bear ourselves that, if the British Empire
and its Commonwealth
Last for a thousand years, men will still say
"This was their finest hour".'

***Again, on 20 August 1940
to the House of Commons he said:***

'The gratitude of every home in our island, in our
Empire, and indeed throughout the world,
Except in the abodes of the guilty,
goes out to the British airmen who,
Undaunted by odds, unwearied by their constant
challenge and mortal danger,
Are turning the tide of war by their prowess
and by their devotion'.

And then he said those immortal words:

*'Never in the field of human conflict was so much owed by
so many to so few'.*

*The picture of Dot, Flo and I carried by dad
throughout the war*

The Easter Bombings 1941

Good Friday 11 April 1941 was a Christian holiday
Commemorating the crucifixion of our Lord, Jesus Christ
And of his death on that cross on the hill at Calvary
But that did not stop the barbarians from bombing
Bristol that night

The Centre, Knowle, Cotham and Filton
were all hammered that night
As the barbarians tried to take out Bristol's
manufacturing might
Trams so badly damaged, Bristol Tramways
permanently closed
And now there was little transport to travel on deadly,
treacherous roads

Winston Churchill visited the ruins on 12 April 1941
Everyone realised that the softening up
had really begun
How long before marauding, invading armies
finally arrived
If they got to our house, we would not be alive

Mum confided in me, secretly, many years later
That she had a plan to frustrate that evil dictator
No way would she allow the Jerrys to abuse us
With gas from our oven, whilst in our beds,
she would kill us

Is it any wonder that she suffered from PTSD?
The decisions she contemplated were the worst
they could be
The tales that she heard about those
despicable invaders
She must have felt that if they reached us,
then nothing could save her

The last night raid on Bristol was on 25 April 1941
When Brislington, Bedminster and Knowle
were bombed
They missed their target of the Filton's
manufacturing areas
So, lucky for us, we missed being harmed

Let us just stop for a moment and reflect on the scene
What a terrible trauma those days must have been
Three children to care for and one on the way
And whether our Dad would return to us,
no-one could say

Mum was concerned at our safety, at our health,
and at home
And instructed us firmly not far away to roam
If you see any aircraft, then please be fleet
For the Germans shoot and kill children:
right here in the street

Listen carefully to the aircrafts' engines and
then you will know
Think: is it our friends, or is it the foe?
That low woo, woo, woo, sound is clearly the Germans
Quickly into the house please go, go, JUST GO!

Each a little incident like the prick of a pin
The food just got scarcer; the people got thin
The cold weather chilled your bones to the core
And her nerves, totally frayed,
she could not take much more.

Wartime Fashion Rationing

Even fashion was rationed: for all of us a chore
Nice clothes, nice shoes available no more
Improvisation was the motto going around at the time
Make do and mend, and we will all be just fine

Producing uniforms and clothing for the troops,
all were hell bent
And out to the Western Front for our boys
they were sent
Nothing was wasted, even if worth less
than a farthing
Women spent hours on repairing, replacing,
knitting, and darning

Cartoon character Mrs Sew and Sew,
gave out some very handy tips
Turning collars, darning socks,
even moth holes could be fixed
Fortunately, Butter muslin was not rationed:
good cloth for making undies
Working seven days a week,
including Saturdays and Sundays

Stockings were scarce, unless you were
friendly with the Yanks
And you can guess what they wanted as a way
to say thanks!
Over here, overpaid, and oversexed it was said
And they tried their damned hardest to get
you into bed

The Government issued a booklet to all young and old
How to repair and revive worn out clothes,
this they were told
Old jumpers and cardigans could have the wool rewound
And converted to other clothes: good use all round

Granny Croome asked her sons to send
home parachute silk
Recovered from war scenes? she could not
have cared zilch
Whilst I wrote to Uncle Bill a little note that said:
'Please send me a camel, but not one that's dead'!

Dances and parties in abundance were found
And girls started to enjoy themselves with the GIs in town
If no stockings were available, then gravy
browning was used
For a line from the bottom of their knickers
to the backs of their shoes

Wartime and Carpet Bombing: 1941

Hitler decided to carpet bomb our country
To destroy our heritage, slaughter our inhabitants
To browbeat us down until we all surrendered
He did not care if they were adults, children, or infants

Our cathedrals, our churches, our hospitals, our schools
Our houses, our museums, our libraries, our pools
Everything that makes a civilised nation
Eradicate them all, was his dire intention

The Nazis had no time for opposing civilisations,
Destroy the moral and structure, of every opposing nation
Coventry, Hull, London, Cherbourg, and more
Le Havre, Lorient, Rotterdam, and Malta:
flatten to the floor

Did these airmen have a conscience I wonder
Bombing civilians and destroying their homes
Killing adults, children, and babies
Bombing us relentlessly, zone by zone

Fear is a terrible thing, it is sure
It stays with you constantly, it gnaws at your soul
Sometimes the fear is groundless, but it feels just as real
Day, after day, after day: it makes you feel ill

The Nazis are coming, they are brutal and cruel
Over the whole world their intention is to conquer and rule
The jackboots are cracking down with power and might
The entire world is in such a terrible plight

Let me address those idiots that say
"We should not have bombed Dresden and
Hamburg that way,"
Why not? Right until the very end London
was faced with V2s
Would Hitler have carried on living if any
chance he wouldn't lose?

We owe a debt of gratitude to Grandad and
our other relatives
For reasons not able to go off to fight in the war
They supported our family without reservation
Nothing for them was too difficult or a step too far

Three houses in Wilton Close were demolished that night
Death and destruction a terrible sight
The blast was so bad, our house was not spared
Blown out windows, collapsed ceilings,
by god we were scared

Can you even imagine, how Mum must have felt?
No husband on hand to give her support
Many a person would have just fallen on their sword
Was it cruel to bring a baby into this terrible world?

Bombings continued night after night
People were living in terrible plight
Each morning revealed new destruction and despair
Caused by those sub-humans who bombed from the air

Ted remembers the night that his Dad found the bomb
Laying in the garden, how could he keep calm?
The disposal squad came, and they took it away
And they were saved to fight for another tough day

The School Run:
Mum faces terrifying bombing

Doncaster Road Infants' School was newly constructed.
In September young Florence began being taught there
So, for Mum two young children going to
two different schools
And with me under 12 months old, dreadful,
it broke all the rules

In early summer of 1940 Mum found out that
she was pregnant
Something apparently not expected and
definitely not planned
An additional worry since war was progressing
And the Nazis were preparing to invade our great land

Filton Airfield was a primary target,
when the bombings commenced
Any time of the day or of the night an attack
could be sent
No morals, no ethics no care for civilisation
Hell bent on destroying our heroic nation

Women and children were fair targets for their games
In the homes, in the streets, or in schoolground,
all the same
Children had to be taught safety:
wartime commonsense
If you hear those engines throbbing,
you know their intent

Kids listen to the aircraft engines, is it friend or is it foe?
That low pulsing sound is clearly German,
'into the house: quickly go!'
Please do not hesitate, please be fleet
Those scum will even shoot children,
right there in the street.

Mum never knew when she left her children at school
Whether she would see them again, if at all
The invaders were getting so much closer: so near
The worry, the tension the overpowering fear

When the war ended certain people would say
How can you treat these poor German people that way?
You were not there, you don't know, you haven't a clue
To destroy every Nazi was the least we could do

Wartime propaganda: Lord Haw-Haw:
The traitor William Joyce

Things were made much worse by
Lord Haw-Haw the traitor
Born to British parents in the US of A,
Moved to Ireland at the tender age of three, and then later
Educated in England, how ironic could that be?

Enthralled with fascism and a Nazi at heart
And a deep hatred of communism, right from the start
He joined Oswald Mosley's British Union of Fascists in 1932
But was sacked by them, so now what could he do?

Furious, he split off from the British Union of Fascists
And founded his own party, the National Socialist League
More virulently anti-Semitic than the other parties
Allegedly, integration into German Nazism was
British society's need

Joyce began broadcasting false news and Nazi propaganda
Had he been caught we British would have torn him apart
So, he travelled to Germany with his second wife, Margaret
And his dirty work for the Nazis in Berlin was about,
in earnest, to start

Joseph Goebbels' Reich Ministry of Propaganda was delighted,
And gave William Joyce his own radio show,
"Germany Calling", Germany Calling"
spread Nazi propaganda to Allied countries,
Especially to Britain and America, his broadcasts would go

His initial broadcasts were aimed at inciting
the nation's distrust,
And to convince us that we were being oppressed,
By the upper class, and by Jewish businessmen
By which the government was mainly controlled

He used the characters Schmidt and Smith
to undermine British people
Degrading and attacking them at every chance
The wealthy and privileged classes were
his main targets
They controlled big business, the newspapers
and led us a dance.

His caustic rhetoric, and upper-class tone
initially appealed to British audiences back home
His fiery oratory more entertaining than most,
His sneering speech degrading, his former English host.

And so, the moniker of Lord Haw-Haw came about
Even though he was little more than a lout
At first people loved him and thought he was fun
But then as the war progressed, his reputation was gone

*A traitor, a scumbag, a rogue, a charlatan: with a nasally up-
per-class English accent. A back-stabber: the nicest about him
that I can bring myself to say!*

The Night the Ceiling came down:
(Good Friday 11 April 1941 bombing)

Good Friday is supposed to be a day of solemn reflection
But not in 1941, when Germans bombed our nation
They did not care who they injured or killed
Or if their bombs fell on a factory, a home or a field

The Good Friday bombings were ferocious and cruel
The Nazis were coming, of that she was sure
The threat of gassing was very intense
On our complete annihilation, the Germans were hell bent.

Gas mask drills were the order of the day
As my grandfather would, sarcastically say
The bastards used gas in that terrible Great War
Killing and maiming men, that's what I saw

We owe a debt of gratitude to Grandad and other relatives
Not destined to go off to fight in the war
They supported our family, without reservation
Nothing for them was ever a step too far

Houses continued to be bombed, come what may
Windows were blown out day after day
People struggled to make repairs whatever the weather
All we could do was pray and stick together

Can you even imagine, how mum must have felt?
No husband on hand to support her,
what a blow had been dealt
How distressed she must have been, the worry, the fear
Bringing a fourth child into this terrible world,
with her dear Fred not near

Bombings continued night after night
People were living in terrible fright
Each morning revealed new destruction and despair
From those sub-humans who bombed from the air

Each little incident like the prick of a pin
The food just got scarcer; the people got thin
The cold weather chilled your bones to the core
And her nerves, totally frayed,
she could not take much more

The terrifying Easter night Peter was born (Sunday 13 April 1941)

So, Mum became head of the family
Alone and clearly frightened to death
And then came a surprise that simply stunned her
Dad had made her pregnant before he had left

By Easter weekend my Mum was heavily pregnant,
And into the air raid shelter she found it impossible to get
And so, the favourite place to hide was under the bed
Brought downstairs, placed on bricks and into
the front room was set

My mum suffered badly during her confinement
An easy birth it was not to be
She struggled on gamely, still trying to look after us
Not easy when there was already us three

Pregnant and under the greatest war pressure,
She battled to give Peter a life of his own
Until that fateful Sunday, the thirteenth of April
Time to call the midwife, please come quick to our home

Mum's confinement was extremely difficult and distressing
No more children the doctor sternly decreed
Dad was given compassionate leave
to come home and visit us
Hey kids: look after your Mum and don't cause a fuss

When Peter was born it was during the nighttime
And next morning my aunty Vi whispered to me
'Come downstairs and see your new little brother
You will love him, I am sure, that I can see.'

Seventy-seven years later, I still visualise that scene so well
The bed in the front room, and Mum looking so pale
But I had a brand-new little brother, and his name was Peter,
And life should have got an awful lot sweeter

And although many miles now separate us today,
Our bond is still close to in every single way
Together we would grow and would argue and would play
Whilst struggling to keep the Nazis away

It was good that Dad was allowed home on
compassionate leave
But in some ways, this really did heighten the pain
In a very short time, he was compelled to depart again
The sadness of parting so hard to believe

Dad is Going Abroad to War

Then came the very, very sad day,
her dearest Fred was going away
And the chance was, it might be forever
She remembered the war of the last generation
And of the slaughter of the very young of the nation.

Dad was called up to serve in the Royal Air Force
He worked as a driver and motor mechanic
He was stationed quite close and so managed to get home.
Here he could help Mum and ameliorate her panic

He got to servicing the Wing Commander's favourite car
And this man did not want Dad travelling too far
And so was kept on the station for a little bit longer
Which benefited everyone and kept Mum a bit stronger.

This initial posting had turned out
to been quite helpful indeed
During those first couple of months,
he was so safe and secure
But now he was going far, far away into danger,
not her need
Where to and for how long, no one was sure

After Dad returned from compassionate leave
to his camp, in tears
He was sent overseas, and we did not see him again,
for nearly five years
He was attached to the Eighth Army under his
hero Montgomery
A soldier who treated all his men with compassion
and humility

I remember the day, that Dad went away
Even though I was just only three
Mum lifted me up and said give Dad a kiss
All of us are going to miss him, much more after this

I am told by my mum that I cried for five days
I sat in the window looking at the street, both ways
No matter what she told me I couldn't be appeased
I want my Daddy, please, please, please, please.

The bad news came through that the Germans
were advancing
And they had their sights on our precious green land
This was the stuff of bad dreams, horrors,
and nightmares
Stop: or we will fight to the death,
was our government's demand

To Egypt and Cairo which he did not like very much
He deeply mistrusted the Arabs, a dirty smelly bunch
Who were always out to steal money,jewellery, and food
And to all the troops they were servile, but extremely rude

By boat to Sardinia and then all around the Med
And then on to North Africa, the desert war, many were dead
Down to South Africa next, and then on to Durban
After the war, he said, here I shall be returning.

Can you imagine Mum's state of emotions?
And how distressed and dismayed that she must have felt
Bringing a tiny baby into this terrible situation
With no certain future: what a very tough hand to be dealt

Each little incident like the prick of a pin
The food just got scarcer; the people got thin
The cold weather chilled your bones thro' to the core
And her nerves, totally frayed,
she could not take much more

The Germans had a mini battleship called the
Admiral Graf Spee
Which was feared by our merchant shipping, every single day
Churchill sent the Ajax, Achilles and Exeter,
the pride of our fleet
Sink her and the battle of the River Plate
would soon be complete.

This was the first naval battle of the Second World War
Taking place in September off the South American shore
Uruguay was neutral and would not give it shelter
When the ship entered the port of Montevideo

The battle was furious, much damage was done
The Exeter, severely damaged, was forced back to her home
The Captain of the Grafs Bay, finding his ship
damaged and trapped,
In the mouth of the River Plate, scuttled the vessel
to avoid capture, what a rat!

But this was just a prelude to very hard times to come
The battle of the Atlantic would see further war crimes done
As the Germans did not care what or who they sent
to the bottom
Women and children and wounded they sank;
Nazis were rotten

The U boats were initially very successful
Dreadful opponents of our brave merchant fleet
But without the food that our heroic sailors brought us
We would have starved: even less food for us to eat

Each little incident like the prick of a pin
The food just got scarcer; the people got thin
The cold weather chilled your bones thro' to the core
And your nerves, totally frayed, could you take much more?

The sinking of HMS Hood

On 24 May 1941 came the Battle of Denmark Strait
or Operation Rheinübung
A naval engagement between ships of the Royal Navy
and the Kriegsmarine
The German ships were attempting to break out
into the North Atlantic
To attack Allied merchant shipping: that was their scene

The British battleship HMS Prince of Wales
and the battlecruiser HMS Hood
Fought the German battleship Bismarck
and the heavy cruiser Prinz Eugen,
Less than 10 minutes after the British had opened fire,
A shell from the Bismarck struck HMS Hood near her
aft ammunition magazines

HMS Hood exploded and sank within three minutes,
The shock: 1,415 of her crew were lost, only three survived
The Prince of Wales continued to exchange fire,
but soon broke off the engagement
A disaster of massive proportions was what was declared

Florrie Watts was Granny Brooks's neighbour
in St. George's House in Bristol
Where they all hid in their flats from the bombing,
all quiet and good
When Florrie burst into granny's flat, sobbing and screaming
I have just been informed: My husband has died, he
went down with the Hood

Gran's brother Shadrack and now her best friend's
husband, both lost in the war
Less than two years since it started, so how many more?
And slowly Granny Brooks was losing the use of her sight
The world and our family in a terrible plight

Each little incident like the prick of a pin
The news was just terrible; the people were scared
The threats from abroad chilled your bones to the core
And Mum's nerves, totally frayed,
she could not take much more

The Japanese attack on Pearl Harbour:
8 December 1941

Just as we were beginning to think that the war
we could not win
A miracle happened: The Empire of Japan
committed a sin
They decided to bomb the Americans,
right out of the war
They got it wrong; every American was disgusted,
bitter and sore

***Below is the famous speech heard by millions of
shocked Americans over their radios that day:***

"Yesterday, December 7, 1941 – a date which will live
in infamy – the United States of America was suddenly
and deliberately attacked by naval and air forces of the
Empire of Japan. The United States was at peace with
that nation and, at the solicitation of Japan, was still
in conversation with its Government and its Emperor
looking toward the maintenance of peace in the Pacific.

Indeed, one hour after Japanese air squadrons had com-
menced bombing in Oahu, the Japanese Ambassador
to the United States and his colleague delivered to the
Secretary of State a formal reply to a recent American
message. While this reply stated that it seemed useless
to continue the existing diplomatic negotiations, it con-
tained no threat or hint of war or armed attack.

It will be recorded that the distance of Hawaii from Japan makes it obvious that the attack was deliberately planned many days or even weeks ago. During the intervening time the Japanese Government had deliberately sought to deceive the United States by false statements and expressions of hope for continued peace.

The attack yesterday on the Hawaiian Islands has caused severe damage to American naval and military forces. Very many American lives have been lost. In addition, American ships have been reported torpedoed on the high seas between San Francisco and Honolulu.

Yesterday the Japanese Government also launched an attack against Malaya.

Last night Japanese forces attacked Hong Kong. Last night Japanese forces attacked Guam. Last night Japanese forces attacked the Philippine Islands. Last night the Japanese attacked Wake Island. This morning the Japanese attacked Midway Island. Japan has, therefore, undertaken a surprise offensive extending throughout the Pacific area. The facts of yesterday speak for themselves.

The people of the United States have already formed their opinions and well understand the implications to the very life and safety of our nation. As Commander-in-Chief of the Army and Navy, I have directed that all measures be taken for our defence.

Always will we remember the character of the onslaught against us. No matter how long it may take us to overcome this premeditated invasion, the American people in their righteous might will win through to absolute victory. I believe I interpret the will of the Congress and of the people when I assert that we will not only defend ourselves to the uttermost but will make very certain that this form of treachery shall never endanger us again.

Hostilities exist. There is no blinking at the fact that our people, our territory and our interests are in grave danger. With confidence in our armed forces – with the unbounded determination of our people – we will gain the inevitable triumph – so help us God.

I ask that Congress declare that since the unprovoked and dastardly attack by Japan on Sunday, December seventh, a state of war has existed between the United States and the Japanese Empire".

President Franklin Delano Roosevelt, December 8, 1941.

As the President had requested, Congress voted, and war was declared on Japan.

The Yanks are coming

The Americans are coming, the Yanks are coming
With nylons and chocolates and goodies galore
The Germans will soon have their backs to the wall
There is now a good chance that we might win the war

Each little incident like the prick of a pin
The food just got scarcer; the people got thin
The cold weather chilled your bones to the core
But with the help of the Yanks, perhaps we need
not take much more.

Most of the world's countries, including all the great powers, eventually formed two opposing military alliances: The Allies and the Axis.

To Dorothy. wishing you a merry
X mas and happy new year with love
your loving father
x x x x x x x

Christmas cards from dad who was fighting in Sardinia 1942

To 76 wishing you a merry X-mass and happy new year with love
your loving Father
x x x x x x x x

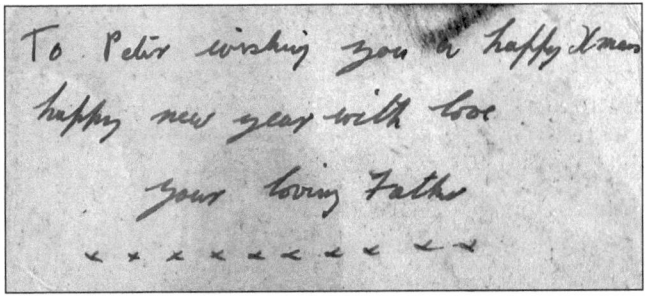

To Peter wishing you a happy X-mas happy new year with love
your loving Father
x x x x x x x x x x

Christmas cards from dad who was fighting in Sardinia 1942

The Family at War: Starvation, Fear, Worry, Anxiety

Bread and sugar, bread, and scrape
From devastating starvation, there is no escape
Endless cold and endless work
There was a war to be won: no one must shirk

During the war my dad travelled all over
Africa, Egypt, the Mediterranean and more
My Uncle Bill was in Egypt, Uncle Stan was in Cyprus
Uncle Vern was in Germany: a prisoner of war.

On D Day Uncle Arthur landed on Gold Beach,
What courage; a hero to us, one and all
When disembarking from the landing craft
he sank beneath the waves
His taller comrades hoisted him up and, thankfully,
by luck was saved

Uncle George was a fireman at the BAC Filton Airfield,
In those relentless day and night raids many
were killed
On one night two air raid shelters were demolished
by massive bombs
Servicemen and civilians all perished,
but not until years later was this acknowledged

Whilst Uncle Stan was in Cyprus his lorry was ambushed
His best friend who was sitting right next to him was killed
They had travelled in a convoy; that was attacked
by some terrorists
Whose actions were abominable, a crime and a sin.

My Granny Brooks's brother Shadrack was killed
in an air raid
Defending his beloved Bristol, to keep us all safe
Granny was shattered, her world fell to pieces
And she never recovered, it showed in her face

Four children to look after, and money very short
Aged eight years, seven years, two years,
and a new-born
To get them to school was a major event
Neighbours look after each other,
that is what they are for

Mum always kept us spotless, always kept us clean
And dressed as best she could, fashion was not the scheme
Because clothes were strictly rationed,
you needed coupons galore
And their quality not good, of that we were sure

This was her mantra,
which made us all laugh was:

Wash up as far as possible
Wash down as far as possible
Now just wash possible
and now you are all done!

Her legs pedalling her sewing machine all times of the day
Her knitting needles clicking the recycled wool away
Socks darned to within an inch of their life
This was how it was like, to be a war wife

Going to school was chaos and panic
In time, four children in three different schools
Shoes worn out, laces broken and falling to pieces
Stuffed with cardboard to keep out the damp and the cold

These improvisations sufficed in very dry weather,
But when it was winter and ladened with rain
The cardboard was totally soddened and sopping,
The feet all frozen: oh, so much pain

The one delight after returning from the school trip
A cup of hot tea and a well-earned custard cream
Then turn on the wireless: Housewives' choice for a flip
A moment to silently pause and reflect on life's
difficult theme

Incendiary Bombs

Incendiary bombs were what the Germans
had started to use
And they thought that this was a really good ruse
So many buildings made so flimsy, just made of wood
And roofs so vulnerable, against fire: absolutely no good.

So, air raid wardens risked their lives on these roofs
Kicking bombs away very quickly using their hoofs
Or dousing them with water, if any was present
St Mary Redcliffe Church was saved,
by theses heroes' presence

And this strategy was to rebound, just four years later
When the very same type of bombs were used in Japan
Tokyo was totally razed to the ground by our bombers
The whirlwind was reaped, as Churchill had planned

Imminent Danger of invasion

The Nazis are coming, just a few miles away
They could be landing on our beaches later today
Come children quickly, get your gas masks on
Do exactly as I tell you, do nothing wrong.

I know that I sent that horrible man away
When he came with our gas masks, the other day
But what he told us makes very good sense
People dying from gassing, will not help our defence.

Every person must play a most defensive part
To defeat the evil Huns from the very start
To fall at the first hurdle would be a disgrace
**We must stand, we must fight, we must
defend every space.**

Invasion becomes a reality

The Nazis are coming, there is nothing to stop them
They have steamrollered their way across
the battlefields of France
They have swept aside everyone who has opposed them
We really have just a very small chance.

Our last days of freedom are ebbing away
Where do we go to, or should we just stay?
The rumours are saying the Nazis are crude
How can Mum defend her dear little brood?

The only thing stopping them is that little wedge
The English Channel, and they are up to the edge
Paris has fallen, evil Goering has gushed
Within six days the Royal Air Force will be totally crushed

But four things were there to stop them,
as the aerial fighting began
The channel, and guts, and skill,
and devotion of every single man
From the white cliffs of Dover over the beautiful
stretch of blue water,
Those incredible few are waiting to stop a bloody slaughter

The Nazis are coming, they are ruthless and cruel
They will even shoot soldiers with their backs to the wall
Civilised conventions are rubbish they say
We will destroy you whichever, or which way

The hopes and dreams of all of us, evaporating slowly
The memories of the last war encroaching daily
The atrocities of the Nazis so clearly remembered
The sights of bodies so cruelly dismembered.

The threat of German paratroopers landing on our shores
Used with very great effect against Belgium and Holland
Our ever-vigilant Home Guard patrolling the beaches
and uplands
Watching the skies, fearful of being ambushed

Our complete brood with Peter that mum had to look after 1943.

Mum shows the first signs of stress

Grandad Brooks was a great support whilst dad was away
From Hotwells to Southmead he cycled many a day
A difficult hilly and long journey, in sunshine and rain
And by then over sixty, he was sure feeling the pain

He built her a chicken run for our one-day old chicks
Made from wire netting and various old wooden pegs
Until then they had grown in the airing cupboard,
next to warm bricks
Until they needed more space to exercise their legs

They grew into chickens to provide us with food
Eggs for our breakfast, and omelettes so good
And sadly, at Christmas one would just disappear
To appear on our table, to give us some cheer

The result of this pressure was a very sad event
Something happened which was not really meant
My Mum loved our grandad, always joking around
They loved each other dearly: their relationship was sound

Then out of the blue, one very sad day
My Mum snapped at something, he innocently said
She shouted at him to leave her alone
In great dismay he went straight off home

My Mother was mortified at the distress she had caused
And apologised profusely, the next time they met
She could not understand what had come over her, she said
Both her and Grandad were so very upset

They both spoke honestly of what had gone on
Mum had no explanation for the change in her moods
She did not want Grandad to stop being jokey
I do not know what came over me she sadly said

And so, Grandad helped us in a great many ways
And Mum despaired at the way she had behaved
Oh, please forgive me she frequently said
Something is messing about with my head

The 'V' 2 Bombs and Doodlebugs

Just when we thought that the blitz was past
Our country was subjected to ferocious bomb blasts
A frightening new weapon rained down from the skies
Killing and maiming and frightening and sighs

A terrifying new weapon Hitler had created
A flying bomb, a buzz bomb, or a doodlebug, it was stated
The German's Revenge weapon, the V1 was born
To grind us into the dust was what Hitler had sworn

More than 6,000 killed, over 18,000 injured
The scale of destruction was truly amazing
Our pilots tried hard to destroy these jet missiles
But Hitler was intent on reversing the war

They travelled at over 400 miles per hour
Containing high explosives, and a tiny propeller
When the scheduled number of rotations was reached
The missile would plummet on town, farm or beach

No sound did these missiles make as they descended
No warning to take cover or hide from the foe
The moral of the people once more took a hiding
And Hitler was again in the ascent and high riding.

Fortunately, the launch sites had to be close to our coast
For the missiles to reach us and turn us to toast
But our brave troops were advancing by day and by night
And destroyed every single weapon and site

But only just in time was the destruction
of missile sites done
One million evacuees from our capital had begun
Women and children, elderly and disabled
Were herded away, bagged up and labelled

So once again our beloved land was saved
By anti-aircraft guns, Spitfires, Hurricanes,
and fighters' brave
Pilots and gunners who put their lives on the line
So that we could survive for yet another time

Every Sunday of every week of every year that
Dad was away
Mum would lift us up onto the sideboard
and lovingly say
Please kiss the photo of the man we all adore
Dressed in his uniform and RAF cap, a hero for sure

And on every Christmas, there was an extra special kiss
Together with a very special heartfelt wish
Let us all pray fervently that this time next year
Dad will be sharing our Christmas right here.

Dad on his motorbike taken in Asmara,
Ethiopia before his accident.

Mum gets a Telegram from the War Office

The news from the front made us further dismayed
Of a visit from the telegram boy, we were always afraid
Dressed in his uniform with little black hat
And a small leather bag: a mark of his trade

And he brought the message that every wife dreaded
Our Dad had become a serious casualty of war
Was he dead, alive, how bad was he injured?
Would he survive to see us all just once more?

Dad was the sole survivor of a terrible tent fire
The lone survivor of a team of six men
Five died in the tent fire in the middle of that desert
Dad, stood in the doorway, blown out
and escaped with his life

I now know the reason why that tent exploded
Dad told me in secret, many years later
In trying to escape the torment of small flies and creatures
A ditch around the tent was carefully excavated

Against all rules this trench was filled with petrol
This kept the insects and mosquitos away
But how a cigarette butt came to ignite it
No one will ever know to this day

Dad was in hospital for many long weeks
In agony from the terrible burns, he had suffered
His complete back, his neck and head scorched
by the flames
But alive, although for a long time in terrible pain

An inquiry was held to determine the causes
Dad could only guess at what had started the fire
From either outside or inside the tent he suspected
A cigarette butt still alight was ejected

He kept his counsel to protect what he knew
And to avoid blame being placed on a mate
A guilty verdict would be a complete disaster
For his family would suffer, lose any pension,
as part of his fate

This was a major incident, far greater than
the prick of a pin
But one thing consoled her, in hospital he was safe
Away from the front line, less chance of being killed
Still, her nerves, totally frayed, she was still unfulfilled

Our wartime Christmas stocking

The one thing Mum insisted on, despite all the strife
She would give us a good Christmas: religion was her life
She would take us to Bristol Cathedral,
where from under the Christmas tree
Mince pies and chocolates and a present each:
all for free

We would make our own decorations out of coloured
paper, stuck down with starch
The gas boiler would be lit, the warmth was a good start
We would all help to stir the Christmas puddings,
and lick the big spoon
And then hang pre-war decorations in
our festive front room

When we woke on Christmas morning,
much earlier than Mum wanted
A huge Christmas stocking for each
on the corner of the beds
Each containing an orange, an apple, some nuts,
some sweets, and a toy
Dot and Flo's naturally, a little different from us two boys

My best present ever was a battleship made of wood
Carved by an Italian Prisoner of War, it was so good
Three deep red funnels that could be taken out and stored
And miniature guns in many places:
how else to fight the war

Letters home from the men at the Front

Letters from troops was a very great lifeline
They came in batches all tied up in string
Mum would sort them, first in date order
And read us the messages, and we could tell,
her heart would just sing

Uncle Bill wrote a letter; is there anything I can send you?
Mum said some parachute silk to make lingerie
And I said 'a camel' and please send it quite quickly
And I can go on a camel racing spree.

Sadly, my camel never arrived at our home
Though Uncle Bill swore that he had sent it by post
I looked for the mail man, with a large humpy parcel
But Bill was still my uncle, and we loved him the most!

The scourge of scarlet fever: 1943

Three children in Ham Green Hospital:
what a terrible plight
Dot and Flo first, and then me, by ambulance,
in the middle of the night
Scarlet fever they said, a most horrible disease
We were kept in isolation until totally cleared for release

Mum was allowed to keep Peter, though ill, at home
You have no one else to infect, as long as you are alone
I watched day after day sandbags being removed
The fear of invasion was over, and they built
a stone wall along the groove

Mum came by bus to pick me up when I was well
We changed buses at the city centre,
and I went under a spell
Mum popped into the bakery and bought
me a sugar-coated bun ring
I scoffed the lot, and the sugar rush
made my heart just go 'ding'.

Mum starts to crack: 1944

And then came an incident etched deep in my memory
What was happening! What was happening?
What a terrible fright!
I'm leaving, I'm leaving, I can take no more of it
Mum: Shouting and yelling in the middle of the night

My mother had spoken, her will had been broken
We all feared for what she would do next
But she recovered her composure,
and hugged us up close to her
And said she was so sorry, she had been so terribly vexed

But we were just children, ignorant and unknowing,
Of the traumas she was suffering and aching inside
We still could be naughty, she could also be haughty
But we knew there were problems, from that she could
not hide.

The fact I remember the incident, some eighty years later
And the memory it burnt deep inside of my mind
Now reminds me of the terrors and horrors she suffered
With four little children left alone and behind

Each little incident like the prick of a pin
The food just got scarcer; the people got thin
The cold weather chilled your bones thro' to the core
And your nerves, totally frayed, could not take much more

Mum, the headmaster
and that haircut: 1944

I came home one day with a note from my headmaster
Telling my Mum that my hair was a disaster
She stormed out the house, straight up to the school
To tell that stupid idiot not to be such a fool.

Money was very short, as it was at that time
And she thought that my hair looked just fine
Not like those poor sods with 'Pudding basin' cuts
Who endured the jibes that sent them totally nuts!

I will never know what she actually said
But nothing more about it was heard from the Head
She always prided herself on how good we all looked
I think that his goose was well and truly cooked!

Cinemas and our experiences:

A strike of a match and a small orange flame
Someone was lighting a fag once again
Adding to the smoky and foul-smelling air
The atmosphere in the cinema, a cause for despair

The smoke rose relentlessly as the minutes ticked by
The beam from the projector cutting through up on high
Like a beam from a lighthouse on a dark swirly night
The coughing and barking amplifying the plight

Wrapped in an overcoat with scarf and warm hat
Central heating? Oh yea, that was a laugh!
And in the summer so hot you would almost bake
Why ever did we bother to go, for goodness's sake

The glamorous actresses, the strident first man
Took us away from our cold soulless land
The music and singing could bring tears to our eyes
And at the interval, if lucky, ice cream or meat pies

No plush seats or air-conditioning in those cinema days
But we enjoyed the experience in so many ways
So much laughter and joy, and being scared out of our wits
Even if we ended up, with a hair full of nits!

The Cabot cinema confrontation: 1944

Why are we all waiting out here in the cold?
My four children are all frozen, one just four years old
How can you be so callous and so very cruel?
Giving priority to Italian Prisoners of War

It's Government instructions, the cinema manager replied
Each prisoner must be counted and secured safe inside
And then we will admit you, and get on with the show
The prisoners are entitled to some leisure you know!

My Mum went ballistic, she was seething with rage
My Dad was a POW in Germany and barely survived
Starved to a skeleton, worked till he dropped
And you ask us to wait for those evil, Hitler loving Whops?

The mood in the cinema was tense and no fun
Particularly when she heard the comments when
the Newsreel was run
How can they support Hitler, that dastardly Hun?
There is sure to be some reckoning when this war is all done

Glen Miller is dead: 15 December 1944

Mum loved her music, particularly dance music
And one great solace was listening to big bands in a trance
With friends and relations, they would move
back the furniture
And in the absence of men, the women would dance

Joe Loss, Victor Sylvester, Glen Miller and more
Were on the radio with sensational scores
And provided the music to alleviate the tension
And help them to survive this despicable war

Glen Miller joined the US Army and they started to sway
He jazzed up the marching tunes: they are still used today
They were also immensely popular with the German troops
So, Hitler banned them, a spoilsport and a terrible poop!

And then came the sad news, Glen Miller was missing
His plane left for Paris to play a liberation concert there
The nation held their breath, please let him survive
They think his plane crashed in the channel,
swept away by the tide

Mum was in tears as she told us that day
Glen Miller is dead, he has now gone away
No longer will we dance to his swinging tunes
One minute happy, then sad: far too soon.

The moral of the nation took a dive that day
Although an American, to our soldiers he would play
His swinging march music, an uplifting sound
And sadly, no body to bury in the ground.

Many years later and conspiracy theories still abound
Was he a spy, why was he not found?
Did he die from lung cancer? He was constantly smoking?
Or was it just an accident,
killed by friendly jettisoned bombs?

The Battle of the Bulge: 16 December 1944

Hope then despair, hope and despair
There are grounds for optimism, victory is in the air
Then comes the news of another insurgence
And the Germans are staging another emergence

Just as the battle was going our way
Hitler decided that this would be his day
Another offensive, a great Christmas push
He wanted victory badly, it was either win or bust.

A massive Panzer tank involvement, a tremendous surprise
Caught the Yanks unawares, they could not believe their eyes
A fuel depot captured; the prisoners used as human shields
More Nazi atrocities, unarmed prisoners were killed.

No prisoner should delay the advance Hitler decreed,
Interpreted by the savages as not setting them free
They slaughtered 84 of the 125 prisoners they took
Some day these barbarians will be defeated,
and rightly brought to book.

This battle was known as the Ardennes offensive
Soon to be nicknamed the Battle of the Bulge
Called after the line of advance that developed
There seemed nothing that could put the Nazis on hold.

As Pieper and his columns swept through Belgium villages
Driving out the Americans and pillaging the towns
Murdering over 100 innocent civilians
Their sickening atrocities knew absolutely no bounds

The Panzer Divisions were in the front lines
And with arrogance they thought that they were doing fine
But they were unaware of proximity fuses
A secret design: one of America's ruses

These ensured that shells exploded above the ground
Causing major destruction all around
And with bridges being blown up in front of the advance
The Nazis suddenly realised;
they had taken a terrible chance.

On Elsenborn Ridge, the Americans dug in
This was the grandstand they were determined to win
Fox holes dug into the solid rock using TNT
To lose this vantage point just wasn't to be

With Patton and Eisenhower and Montgomery encamped
They developed a plan to stop the advance
But heavy snowstorms stopped any aircraft support
And freezing cold weather brought troops to a halt

Then on Christmas Eve the skies cleared, and clouds lifted
The allied planes poured in with much needed supplies
Food, ammunition, clothing and medicines
Medics, reinforcements, a sight for sore eyes.

Some Germans by now had reached the river Meuse
But became isolated, for them, very bad news
On Boxing Day Patton broke into the bulge
And reinforced his troops, who had been trapped
and unable to move.

Hitler now realised that the battle was lost
But tried to give the dice one more serious toss
On New Year's Day the Luftwaffe launched a massive attack
It failed, and that was the end: Ho, HO, HO
what a terrible loss!

Two hundred Allied planes destroyed in the battle
But Germany lost 350 or more
Germans were retreating, most realised it was over
The Battle of the Bulge, which almost defeated us,
was now secure.

By 25 January 1945 the battle was over
Hitler's last cast of the die had certainly been lost
Germans now realised that Hitler was delusional,
And the fight to save Berlin was their final shot

This episode of war was a frightening reminder
That the Nazis would fight to the very last man
Mum's husband and brothers were in the midst
of the mayhem
Where and how they were, she did not have a clue

Although close to defeat, Hitler just would not give up
Yet another new weapon he was planning to release
The V2 or doodlebug a fast, silent rocket
Reaped death and destruction,
and many Londoners were to cop it

Fear and destruction were what Hitler wanted
Women or children, civilians or not
His madness, his evilness, his lack of compassion
If you were not of his beloved race, he did not give a jot

For Mum each event was like a stab in the heart
Brought her endless fear and great distress from the start
When would it all end, when would it be over?
When would her Fred be coming home, no longer a rover?

Elation, Elation, unadulterated elation
Happiness and relief throughout our great land
Our troops will be coming home,
the lights will come on again
And what a Christmas we can look forward to this year

President Roosevelt dies from a heart attack: 13 April 1945

President Roosevelt, a very good friend,
died of a heart attack, so close to the end
Never seeing peace after a war in which his
loyalty was unbounded
This gave Hitler a modicum of hope,
but by 16 April 1945 he was surrounded
And the final assault on the government
buildings began on 25 April 1945.

The battle for Berlin: April 1945

On 30 April 1945 the centre of Berlin was reached,
by the Russians
Who blasted the German Nazi Powerhouse with
huge guns at point blank range
Four hours later the Russian Red Flag was raised
above the roof
And now the war in Europe entered its final phase

Hitler caught like a rat in his underground bunker
There, trapped like an animal down he would hunker
His officers pleaded with Hitler to flee
But he knew he was doomed, whatever his plea

Hitler and Eva Braun commit suicide:
30 April 1945

Hitler successfully tests poison on his favourite dog
Eva Braun finally married Hitler; it had been a long slog
And then she takes poison to end her life
And Hitler shoots himself, not long after
the death of his wife

His Generals tried to broker a surrender to save its face,
But the allies were determined: no way and no place
Only an unconditional surrender was acceptable to the allies
No way out, it was finally accepted, what a surprise!

Victory in Europe: 8 May 1945

7 May at 2.45p.m. the Surrender Document
was finally signed unconditionally,
And the next day was declared 'Victory in Europe (VE) Day
And this is a day I remember well,
there were many emotions and tears
And watching Mrs. Burt waving her Gerry pot:
gone were our fears

And then the war was suddenly over
And Dad would coming be home to stay
There were loads of celebrations and very happy parties,
And strange things that people did and said on that day

The 'V' sign and Florence
is in deep trouble: 1945

I wrote the following lines to explain the situation
Of what my sister Florence did to our council house
All done in sweet innocence, but trouble for Mother
Florence was normally as quite as a mouse:

The war is over hip-hip hooray!
And Winston Churchill has won the day
What can we do, young Florence thought?
To celebrate, we really ought.

After five long years of fighting away
My daddy will be coming home to stay
Something is needed to welcome him back
Something quite special with plenty of crack

I know, she said, it would be cool
To paint Churchill's V sign on a wall
On either side of the front door portals
That will do nicely she gaily chortles

In the shed are pots of paint
But what we don't want is something feint
What we need is something quite bright
What about that tin of white?

Two feet high and one inch thick
That will be so very slick
What about some Morse code too?
Three dots, one dash, that should do

Come out Mum and see my painting
Mum emerges almost fainting
Rules are rules and the Council's pedantic
What can she do, she is totally frantic?

NB. This scene was one I wrote for Meadows to Meaders Episode 3 2020 I was the rent man, and the cast strung washing out in the 'front garden' to disguise Flo's painting and stop the Rent Man from seeing it. We managed to perform it just before Covid and the restrictions descended on us all.

The V Sign still in evidence in 1959.

When Jeanette and I got engaged in June 1959, we had a group photo taken outside our front door. The large V signs and morse code were still clearly visible. Starting from the left: My best friend Ted Hall and his girlfriend Margaret, Jeanette is stood in front of me, my brother Peter stood in front of my mum, friend John Potts.

9 May 1945:
The Channel Islands are liberated

Crowds gathered in the sunshine
in St Peter Port, Guernsey
To welcome the British Task Force sent to
liberate their island
Just in time as the islanders and troops
were very close to starvation
Barely surviving the brutality
of that despicable nation

We get fearful about dad returning home for good

Although we loved our dad,
we had got used to living without him
Dorothy and Flo were entering their teens
Sometimes we were allowed to sleep in mum's bed
You will not be doing that when dad comes home,
Mum quietly said

Mum has an attack of the nerves: 1946

Then suddenly mum found she could just not stop crying
She was in great distress for most of the day
It seemed that even though the situation
had got much easier
People became guarded as to what they could say

There is nothing wrong with me, she frequently said
And yet this sadness is there inside of my head
It appeared that the better our lives became
She seemed to have even more anxiety and pain

I do not know what came over me, I keep upsetting Fred
Recalling an incident, she afterwards said
Something just seemed to burst in my head
If this continues, I would be better off dead

Each little incident like the prick of a pin
The food was much better, the people no longer thin
There was coal for the fire, and clothes to be worn
But her nerves, totally frayed, were tattered, and torn

So back to the Doctors for guidance she went
But they were just useless: get a grip they casually said
The war is over, don't let your energy be spent
And your fears will finally disappear from out of your head

Oh, Mrs Brooks there is really nothing to fear
You are simply suffering from an attack of your nerves
Just enjoy life now that the war is finally over
And forget the past and move on to a forever

To add to her burden, she also endured
A period of painful boils and terrible sores
In embarrassing places, not the thing to discuss
The cure: to sit for hours in a bath of salty water
and cause no fuss

Thankful to God that all her family survived
Mum entered the water and was baptised
She never learnt to swim so head under the water a stress
But she looked so lovely and serene in her simple white dress

Final Memories

Memories of Mum and the struggles she had
Always makes me feel very, so very sad
But through it all she put on a brave face
And always added 'if it is with God Lord's grace'.

If the good Lord spares me, she would often say,
To live until this or that occasion, this or that day
I will do my utmost to be the best that I can
And live out my life with my wonderful man

And every single night her prayers she said,
After thinking of us all, before slipping into bed
Her spiritual beliefs were honest and deep
And she prayed for us all, before going to sleep.

Dad was rewarded by medals galore
To show his input into that terrible war
But Mum got nothing, no recognition, no fame
She just gave all she had in her good Lord's name

Those women who were forced to stay home,
all deserve a gold medal
For what they put up with, whilst their men were away
And though it's too late for her to receive
some acknowledgement,
Posthumous recognition would not go astray!

Just writing this brings a lump to my throat
It always reminds me how she lived life full of hope
Whatever was thrown at her, whatever the die cast
She fought valiantly for her life, to the very, very last

*Mum and Dad: we all loved you to the ends of the earth. I had
to finish this poem at some time but, as you lived for another
47 years, – I have a lot more to say!*

A small pocket calendar of 1945,
that Mum kept in her handbag until the day she died:
a small beacon of hope.

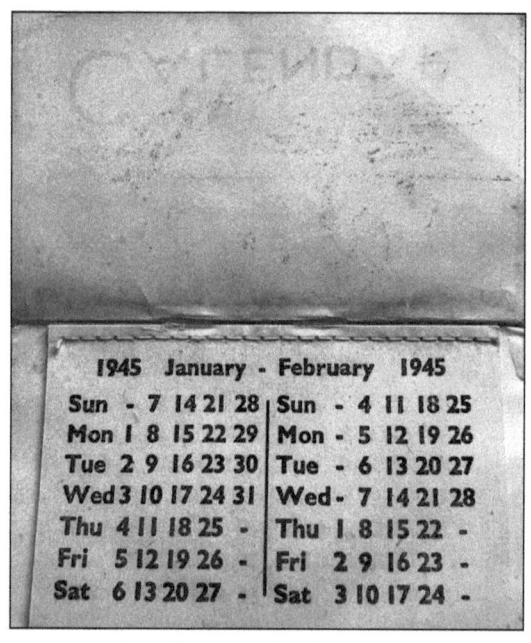

1945	January					-	February				1945
Sun	-	7	14	21	28	Sun	-	4	11	18	25
Mon	1	8	15	22	29	Mon	-	5	12	19	26
Tue	2	9	16	23	30	Tue	-	6	13	20	27
Wed	3	10	17	24	31	Wed	-	7	14	21	28
Thu	4	11	18	25	-	Thu	1	8	15	22	-
Fri	5	12	19	26	-	Fri	2	9	16	23	-
Sat	6	13	20	27	-	Sat	3	10	17	24	-

A small pocket calendar of 1945,
that Mum kept in her handbag until the day she died:
a small beacon of hope.

Mum loved all her grandchildren without reservation and despite all her problems always appeared to be happy. She constantly talked to herself.

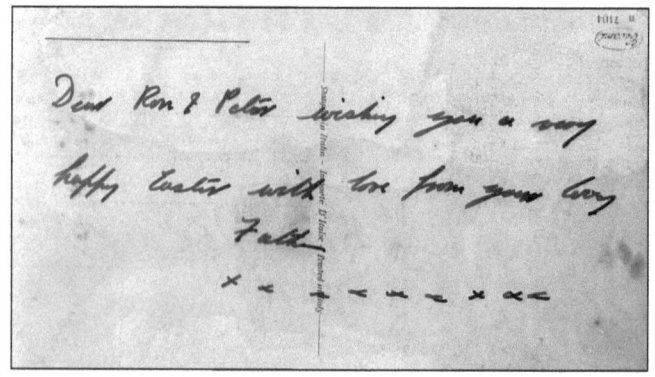

Easter greetings card – To Ron & Pete

Ron Brooks
3 January 2023

Simple Memories

Dedicated to Emily Catherine Florence Brooks
and mainly written by herself.

22nd October 1909 to 7th October 1992

Foreword

When my father died on the 31st of May 1990 my Mother was absolutely devastated. They were married on 20th July 1931 at Bristol Registry Office and the only time they ever spent apart was when dad was in the army during the war and was posted overseas. They were known affectionately by everyone as Em and Fred, and almost always in the same breath.

I was working for Avon County Council at Brislington Depot, Bristol at the time, a short drive from where they lived and so every Wednesday, I would visit them for lunch. After Dad's death I suggested that there were many things that the family did not know about their younger days and asked her to start writing her memories.

By nearly every Wednesday she would have produced a bit more, I would read it, ask more questions and that is how this record of their life together was produced. Aunty Glad would also visit once a month on a Wednesday, so I was able to pick up quite a lot of history from her as well.

Mum died on 7th October 1992 after being taken very ill on the notorious 'Black Wednesday'. She was rushed to the BRI where she died and a big regret is that I was not there, but she was fortunate to have my two sisters: Dorothy (Dot) and Florence (Flo) with her.

These Memoirs were written over this two-year period, and I am certain that it brought her much comfort, satisfaction, and happiness as she recalled her life.

As I read through her story, I am constantly reminded what a happy person she was, and what fun we had as children. This was despite her living through two horrendous wars and the struggle she had bringing up us four children, on her own, with bombings, food shortages and rationing, and never knowing what was happening to Dad, and whether he would ever return safely. Not to forget that she was also pregnant during some of the heaviest bombings and Peter was born on 13th April 1941 when England was virtually alone and on its knees.

The other thing that I am proud of is how well she wrote these pages. Right up to the end her writing is beautiful and easy to read. Her spelling is excellent and the whole document very readable. When you understand that she left school at 12 with not a lot of formal education, it puts many present-day people to shame.

Mum: My name is Emily Croome, and I was born in St. Paul's, Bristol on 22nd October 1909. My mother and father both worked in Allen Davies Printers in Rupert Street. My parents were very happy people, my Dad was very hard working and a wonderful Dad, Mum was very patient and very understanding helping sick people and visiting people who could not do their own shopping.

My Mother's name was Florence Trump before she married my Dad. They first lived in Bloomsbury Buildings, off Charles Street.

My sister Flo was born in 1911 and then my brother Bill was born on 1st September 1915. The First World War broke out in 1914, and my dad was called up for the Army.

We had 'blackouts' at night but no bombs. My Dad was sent abroad to India, and my mother wrote to tell him that she was pregnant with my sister Violet. Vi was born in April and my dad did not see her until she was almost three years old.

He came home from India, had a month's leave and then had to go back to war. Mum did not hear from him for several months. She got in touch with the Red Cross, and they let her know that he was a Prisoner of War in Germany. He was badly treated and when he finally came home from Germany, he was terribly thin, and so ill in himself. After some time being unemployed my Dad managed to get a job in the printer's firm. It meant a lot of travelling to work, but he was a hard worker and never grumbled.

After the war ended, we were allowed very little food, and it was a struggle for my parents, but they were wonderful and often went without supper so that we would have breakfast. When my brother Arthur was born, my mother was very ill and had to go into the BRI (Bristol Royal Infirmary) taking the baby with her. My Dad was out of work, but he well looked after us, and my auntie Nell, Dad's sister, came and done the washing and help Dad as much as possible. My mother was in hospital about a month and when she came home, she needed a lot of care, and we had our little jobs to do after school.

Later my brother Stanley was born, and we were a very happy family, although it was a hard struggle for my parents. When I was five years old, I started school at St.

James School in Stokes Croft. I spent two years there, and then we had to go to North Street School at the age of seven. My parents lived in Moon Street and mum used to wave to us from the window during play time. I really enjoyed my school days. My sister Flo and brother Bill went to the same school, but Arthur and Stanley had to go to Castle Green School.

My Mother was a Roman Catholic, and my Dad was Church of England. Dad wished for all of us to be brought up Church of England but when my youngest brother (Stan) was born he was christened in the Catholic Church. We had so much fun when we were young. My sisters, my other two brothers and myself attended City Road Chapel and on Sundays went three times a day to Sunday school. If you attended Sunday school regularly you went on your Sunday school outings free, but if you missed too often you had to pay a little towards your trip (3d or 6d depending on the number of times you missed going). My mother took us on several outings, the parents paid about 2/6p.

They used to take the parents by coach and the children in a large furniture van. We had forms to sit on, but it was very crowded. I remember going on a trip and we had a wonderful time. We arrived at this big field with swings and a big lake. We had games and then went into a building where we had our tea of jelly, cakes, bread and butter and tea. After tea we would have different races and if you won you had a small gift. We arrived home about 9 o'clock after singing all the way back home. The parents' coach left earlier so that they would be at the church to meet us.

We also went to Christian Endeavour. My sister Vi was a Girl Guide, and my brothers were in the Scouts. Bill and Arthur use to go camping with the Scouts (but not Stan) and I remember once my sister Violet went camping with the Girl Guides. She was so upset being away from home that Mum went to see her at the camp; she wanted to come home, but Mum told her that she would have to wait until Saturday when Mum would meet her off the coach. She never went camping again but continued to go to Guide meetings. Bill and Arthur went on scout outings, but money was very scarce in those days, and she could not always afford to let them go.

At Christmas time we went to the church at about 4 o'clock and had a Christmas tea and after there was a conjuror. Then we had games and when we left we were given a packet of sweets. Whit Sunday was also a special day and we had new shoes and dresses for the girls and new shoes and suits for the boys. We girls always had a new summer hat as you didn't go to church without wearing a hat. It was what you called 'Anniversary Sunday' and we used to practise our singing about three weeks before the special day. City Road Chapel had a wonderful choir, and it was lovely to join in with the choir, especially at Xmas time.

On ordinary Sundays we had to go to the Church Hall and be taught the bible and hymn singing. They had a special children's choir which both my sister Flo and I was in.

Ron: Mum had a good voice and sang a lot at home. If she wasn't singing, she was talking to herself which she did an awful lot. She was a member of Southmead Baptist Church choir, and it was in that church that she was baptised not long after the war ended. She vowed to go through with Baptism if her Dad and all her brothers came home safely from the war. Sadly, she lost her singing voice completely after one of her operations, but thankfully was still able to talk the 'hind legs off a donkey'.

Mum: My father was very strict and if he said that we couldn't do something, he meant it. Mum was very strict also, but both were wonderful and did so much good, especially my Mum in the case of other people's illness.

My mother used to meet us from school and often she would take us, with our tea to spend the evening on Brandon Hill. It was lovely and we played games, and then had our tea of bread and cheese or jam and sometimes a cake. Mum always bought some apples from Allen's Greengrocery shop and after tea we were allowed one apple each. At seven o'clock we went home, had a good wash, then a cup of cocoa and biscuits and then we went to bed. Mum would either sew or knit; Mum and Dad enjoyed these evenings.

When I was 12, I left school and went to work at Allen Davies, the printers in Rupert Street. When my mother took me to be interviewed the man recognised her and I was able to get a job. My sister Flo went into service doing housework, she worked for my boss Mr. Gillett. His wife was very nice, and my sister Flo was very happy there. My brother Bill worked in the printing department at Burleighs in Trenchard Street, but he was not very happy and became a driver on the buses.

My mother's brother Jim (Trump) had a wife called Fanny who was very nice and hardworking. We often went to see her. They lived in Wade Street, near Old Market Street. I remember going with my mother, my sister Flo, Bill and Vi in the pram. (*It must have been round about 1919*). She had a few children and was a wonderful cook. That afternoon she was doing the vegetables for tea and was making a stew. She asked mum if we would like to stay for tea, but Mum said no.

While she was doing the vegetables her little child was sat on the potty. After he was finished Aunt Fanny wiped his bottom and then went straight back to doing the vegetables without washing her hands. Aunt Fanny again asked Mum to stay for tea, my mother made some excuse, and we went home. If only you could have seen the look on my mother's face when she didn't wash her hands!

My Mother and I would never eat anything there after that. Mum was very particular about cleanliness, and we always had to keep ourselves clean and always wash our hands after going to the toilet. When Mum told Dad about the potty, he said he couldn't stand thinking about food, as Dad was also most particular about cleanliness. Uncle Jim and Aunt Fanny died so I don't know any of that family now, but happy memories of past days.

Ron: This might be a repeat of things I have said elsewhere but I shall include it now in any case. Mum was also very particular about cleanliness and kept us, our clothes, and the house scrupulously clean. Every week she would thoroughly scrub the large wooden kitchen table until it was gleaming, and she would also wash and polish the lino in the front room – no carpet in those days. While she was down on her hands and knees, she would let Peter and I take turns at riding on her back.

We were lucky that we had an upstairs bathroom and mum made us all bath regularly. We had a large gas boiler in the kitchen immediately below the bath and Mum would boil water in this. There was a hand pump you lowered into the water and a handle you pushed forwards and backwards to force the water up into the bath above – quite hard work in itself. This boiler was also used to boil up the washing and, best of all, for boiling the Christmas puddings. Mum would often say to us; "wash up as far as possible then wash down as far as possible and then wash possible!

Mum: My mother was a wonderful cook, making Bread Pudding and Spotted Dick (that is a bake mixture with plenty of fruit and boiled in a cloth for about 2 hours) and plenty of pancakes. One Sunday we would have boiled pudding (either bread or Spotted Dick) and the following Sunday rice pudding, so we always knew what was for tea at weekends.

Some evenings we would have a fish and chip supper. Mum would send me and my sister Flo to Jamaica Street for a few 3d lots (of fish and chips). We also had to ask for 'scrumps' which was little bits of batter that had come off the fish and chips. Baldwin's was the name of the fish and chip shop. It was a lovely meal, and we all enjoyed our evening meal and much appreciated it.

Going back to my school days, we had some wonderful times. Mum used to take the youngest child in the pram and go to St. James Park. Behind the park is St James church and opposite the park was the Horsefair. It was so full of beautiful flowers and a gardener was always around. You could not go in unless you were with an adult, but we could play games there. The park opened about 9.00 a.m. and the gates were locked about 6.00 p.m.

They had a round seat at the end of the park with a big tree growing up through the middle. One day coming home from school at about 3.45 p.m. my sisters and I went to meet Mum at the park. A dear old lady came and sat next to my mother, and she was very nice. It was Thursday, the day before Good Friday. The old lady (she would be over 60) asked Mum if she believed in God.

Mum said 'yes' and that she believed in bringing up her family in believing as well.

She told Mum that if on Good Friday you ask the Lord to forgive your sins, you were clearly forgiven, and a new year started free from sin. I always think of her on Good Fridays, and I feel that she was telling the truth. I always remember especially on Good Fridays to ask God to forgive me my past sins and start another year; my sisters think the same way.

Going back to my mother's mother, this was Granny Trump and she had three brothers: Bert, Jim, and Joe. Bert lived at Wilson Street with his cousins. Uncle Joe was a nice man and full of fun and worked very hard. He lived with his daughter, her husband and family near the eye hospital in Maudlin Street. He was taken ill and went into St. Joseph's Home in Cotham (*another Catholic connection?*).

He was there a long time (in the hospital part) and my mother would visit him often, taking one of us with her as only two visitors were allowed. You could only stay for a short time as he was very ill with a cerebral haemorrhage and towards the end, he did not know anyone.

I went in by myself one Sunday and you rang the bell, and a nun would answer it. When you went in the nuns would lock the door after you until you were ready to be let out. The nun was very nice and when I was coming out, she asked me if I would like to see their chapel. It was beautiful and, being near Easter, it was decorated with Arum Lilies and many other beautiful flowers.

She told me to say a prayer and then, when I was leaving, she said that I was really a Catholic. I went home and told my parents, but dad said no, I belong to the Church of England. I was courting Fred at the time and glad that I did not have to change religion as Fred was Protestant and belonged to the Orchard Street Sunday School.

Uncle Joe died and all the grownups went to his funeral at Arnos Vale Cemetery. My Granny Trump missed him very much, but we looked after her and she visited my mother nearly every day. My Granny sometimes got drunk, and my Mum would be very upset about this. She lived in rooms in Stokes Croft and every Sunday my sister Flo and I would take a Sunday dinner to her.

One day she missed a visit to us and so Mum went to see her. Granny Trump had fallen down the stairs and was rushed to the cottage hospital. She had beautiful auburn hair; it was so long she could sit on it. Granny Trump also had a cerebral haemorrhage and the sister told Mum that they would have to operate. The Doctor asked Mum if they could cut Gran's hair as all her strength was in her hair.

Mum gave her permission and when Gran got over the operation, she was so cross with Mum and really swore at her. But her hair grew again, not so long but curly. I've known my Gran to brush her hair sitting on a chair with the hair nearly touching the ground. She was a lovely person, and we enjoyed her company.

My mother and father use to take us to the Pictures when they could afford it. It cost about 3d for children and 6d for grownups. They had the Jack and the Beanstalk picture show on, and my mother took my Gran to see it. My Gran was very scared as the giant was so tall on the screen and Gran thought he was going to walk towards her. She told Mum that she would never go to the pictures again. We all had a good laugh about it, but Granny could not see the funny side of it.

My Granny was a wonderful seamstress, she could make a man's suit, trousers, coats, and waistcoats but she could not do buttonholes. So, the firm used to let Gran take them to Mrs Thomson who lived next door to us in Moon Street. She was paid very well for her work, as she was a war widow and lived with her mother and father Mr and Mrs Cook. They were very good neighbours and very friendly and thought a lot of our family.

My Great Granny Trump
with an abundance of hair

Next door to Mum's was a neighbour, Mrs Pearce. She had a large family of four daughters and three sons, and we all used to go to day school and Sunday school together. Mrs Pearce and Mum were very good friends and went with us on the Sunday school outings.

My sister Flo and I had lovely hair and each night before we went to bed Mum would plait it for us, and next morning would brush our hair and tie our plaits with ribbons. Although we were very poor we were kept beautifully clean and Mrs. Cook our neighbour used to admire the way Mum looked after us. Each night we would have to kneel by the side of the bed and say our prayers: Gentle Jesus meek and mild, look upon a little child. Pity my simplicity and help me Lord to come to thee.

Ron: All four of us children had to do the same routine and words.

Mum: Mrs Pearce tried to do her girl's hair like ours, but the plaits were never curly. Mum tried to do it for them, but the girls' hair always came out strait. We were so happy in our childhood and always had plenty of fun. We would walk miles on Bank holidays going to Durdham Downs or Ashton Park taking our food with us.

My Dad also loved playing football and we would often go to the 'Bristol Downs' to watch him play. Football was always played on Saturday afternoons and Mum would take our tea with us and we would stay until about 7o'clock and then we would walk down Bridge Valley Road, through Hotwells and then home to Stokes Croft.

Ron: Mum thought that Grandad Croome played for Clifton St. Vincent's. Unfortunately, he broke his leg during a match and was off work for some time. In those days there were no welfare benefits and so life was very tough. Granny Croome apparently stopped him from playing football after that.

Mum: Although tram fares were cheap, my parents could not afford to spend money on fares.

Sometimes we would get a treat and walk to where we were going and then ride back on the tram. I think the tram fares were about two or three pence. Small children went free, and we would like to sit on top of the tram. It was lovely and we would wave to all the people.

Some holiday Mondays we would go to the zoo, or we would just go to the 'Downs' and have a picnic. We would have our dinner and then we would walk up Arley Hill and make our way through Redland. We would take our bats and balls and play near the 'dumps'. The youngest then was Violet. It was a lovely spot, and you would jump into small spaces and then just climb up to the top of the dump.

About five o'clock Mum and Dad would say it was time to go home and so we would walk down Blackboy Hill until we came to Clifton Down station. There was a cake shop there, which kept open on holidays. Mum would go in and come out with a large bag of buns and cakes. She would give us one each and we had the rest with our tea when we arrived home. The cakes only cost a few pence in those days and all cakes left over from the previous day were sold off cheaply.

Sometimes on a Saturday we would go to Ashton Park as dad was a Bristol City football supporter. He would go to the City Ground, especially if it was a special match, then meet us in the park. We would then walk through Bedminster and call in to see Auntie Flossie (Dad's sister), have some tea and then happily walk home.

Aunty Flossie lived on Mills Street, a very narrow street but with very nice houses. Dad's other sister, Aunt Nell, also lived with Flossie until she got married and went to St. George to live (Sherbourne Street near the park). She had a lovely wedding. My Mother and Father were invited and we three children who were born then: me, Flo, and Brother Bill.

Flo and I were dressed in our new dresses and white shoes and my brother Bill had a velvet suit. It was a lovely day and so Mum didn't take our coats, not realising that we were going to be so late coming home. We left about 10.30 p.m. and all the trams had finished, so we had to walk all the way home from St. George to Moon Street. Just as we were leaving the place it poured with rain, so some friends lent us some coats.

Dad carried Bill on his shoulders and Flo, and I were wrapped in a large Mack and walked all the way home. We arrived home about midnight, but we had a wonderful time and Mum returned the mackintoshes later. They were all so friendly and we really had a wonderful day.

My Aunt Nell was a very happy person and would do many kindnesses to friends. When my brother Arthur was born, my mother had a very bad confinement and was rushed into the BRI with Milk Fever. She was very ill and Dad's sister, Aunt Nell used to come to our house to help Dad. She gave every help in looking after us. Mum came home and we were so happy to see her and our new brother Arthur.

We had lovely times together and I have so many happy memories of my childhood. After two years Mum had Stanley, my brother. He was brought up in the Catholic religion as Mum wanted one of us to be Catholic and was determined Stan would follow her religion; Dad reluctantly agreed.

When he was five, Stan started school at Trenchard Street. He was happy there, but I don't think he ever understood why he was a Catholic.

He left school when he was 14 and worked in a Butcher's shop, delivering meat to customers. He first started work at Gloucester Road and then he went to work at Cranbrook Road. He loved his job and he used to come to my home at Southmead for dinner Wednesdays and Fridays and we had some good times together.

My friend Mrs Robbins kept chickens and at Christmas time Stan would kill them and take them to the butcher's shop where his boss would pay for them and the money, he gave her helped her very much. My children wanted some rabbits, and I told them that they could have one each if they looked after them and fed them. I must have been kidding myself!

It was OK for a few weeks, and then they forgot to feed them. I told them that if they did not help then I would get rid of the rabbits. I know they loved their pets, but they belonged to different clubs and that was their priority. Ron was in the Scouts and Peter was in the Cubs at Southmead Baptist Church (*The 254 group*).

Stan came to dinner one day and I told him the boys did not want the rabbits. He said not to worry as he could get rid of them. He spoke to his boss, and they had a lady customer and when she heard about the rabbits, she said she would like one. She was so pleased with them and said that she wished we had more to give her.

Then Stan came one Friday, and he killed the rabbit and hung it on the line in the garden until he had finished his dinner. I went out to get him some pudding from the kitchen and the rabbit's head was going round and round. I screamed and Stan came out and said it was just a nerve. He hit it again on the back of the neck and it died. Stan's boss asked him if I was going to have any more and I said: definitely NO as I was really nervous of them.

I started to have baby chickens, but they didn't grow very well, and they seemed to die so quickly. Some young men used to come around the streets with a horse and cart from which they would sell day old chicks at about 1d each. We tried to keep them alive by putting them in a cardboard box in the airing cupboard, which was alongside the fireplace in the front room. We would even heat up a brick on the fire, wrap it in old cloth and put it in with the birds in place of their mother.

A few did survive however, and Fred's Dad cycled up from Hotwells with some timber and wire netting on the handlebars of his bike and built a hen house for them. Mr Hill who lived next door to us in Southmead had two children. His wife had left him, but he was a very nice neighbour. One day he called at our back door and told me he was moving house. He asked if I would like to have a hen and a cockerel as I already had a chicken run.

I fed them on any leftover food mixed up with oats and boiled up. The smell was revolting but I would do anything to keep them alive and produce food as the war had started and everything was on ration. The hen was good at laying eggs. The cockerel was large, and the children used to let him out of the run and ride on his back. I think the cockerel enjoyed it as much as the children. The cockerel was found dead one morning and after that we decided not to have any more chickens

Mr Hill moved out and another family the 'Bridgemans' moved in. They were very noisy and not very clean or wholesome looking. When the mother, Joyce, was moving in she asked Mr. Hill what I was like. He said I was a very good neighbour. She was not married to George at that time, but she told me that they were getting married. After the wedding they asked Fred and me to go around for a drink. Joyce would say that at one time she was a model, and she would walk down the road as if she was on the catwalk.

We went and were shocked to see how dirty her home was. She wanted us to spend the evening with them, but we made our excuses and came back home. I was always friendly to her but didn't like the crowd she mixed with. They had noisy parties at weekends and although many neighbours complained they took no notice.

I was taken to Southmead Hospital on 18th December 1957 and had a major operation for mastoid in the ear. I was very ill and when I came out of hospital in the January the Doctor came to see me. While he was there the noise from next door was terrible. He asked me about them and told me that if the noise did not stop, he would go in to see them.

Fred said that he would go in to see them, and they were much quieter for a while but continued to have so many people there. I think this made me want to move to Smythe Road. I loved my house but with Fred having to do so much travelling and being on call out day and night we decided to move. I missed my house, and I left so many friends behind.

Ron: I remember one occasion just before I went into the forces in 1957 that 'next door' were playing the piano and singing well into the early hours of the morning. The piano was right up against the party wall, and we were unable to sleep. Dad went in to see them and asked them to be quiet. They followed him out of their house shouting abuse at him.

By this time Peter and I were in the window to see what was happening and so were Peter Osborne and his family who lived right opposite. It was obvious that the Osbornes were also unhappy with the racket the Bridgemans were making.

George Bridgeman suddenly spotted the Osbornes during his rant. They were big lads and not afraid of anyone and George quickly went indoors. I spoke to Peter Osborne the next day and he said that him and his brothers were just about to come down to sort George out, because all the immediate neighbours were totally fed up with their behaviour.

Mum: Apart from them, all the time we lived at Southmead we had very good neighbours. I had a good friend Mrs Parfitt who had a daughter Beryl. The children used to play together and got on very well with each other. Mrs Parfitt had a second baby, but it died.

Mr Parfitt was also very nice and hardworking, and he would cycle to and from work every day, arriving back home about 5.30 p.m. One evening he was late in coming home and Mrs Parfitt was so worried as he was always punctual.

Later in the evening a policeman called to tell her that her husband had a heart attack on his way home and he died near Horfield Common. It was a terrible shock to us all. Mrs Parfitt continued to live in Coleford Road for many years, Beryl got married and then Mrs Parfitt moved, and we lost touch with each other.

Ron: I remember this incident well and apparently Mr Parfitt would always cycle right to the top of Toronto Road, which is quite steep, even though his friends would get off and walk the last part of the hill. Apparently, some had warned him, but he did not take heed.

Mum: Mrs McCarthy was another of our neighbours and she became our post woman. She would walk down the street reading any post cards that had been sent and would tell us what was in them before we had a chance to read them ourselves. She would keep her coal in the bath, which in the terrace houses was downstairs, because she said that they did not believe in taking baths!

I worked for Allen Davies's for seven years. When I was sixteen, I met my husband, Fred. His Auntie, Mrs Smith, lived near us. She introduced me to Fred, and we went out for a few weeks, but my parents said I was too young.

I started courting him again when I was seventeen and a half years old. Fred and I were very happy together. He worked very often at weekends, and I had to go to Sunday afternoon and evening services at City Road Chapel. I loved it there and went to 'Christian Endeavour' every Monday. When Fred was not working Sundays, we always went to Chapel.

Fred's mother, father and three sisters lived at 9 Pipe Lane for many years. Then they moved to a flat in St. George's House, Hotwells, which was at that time right opposite the garage. They were right at the top of the building with a lot of stairs to go up. They had to carry everything up there including coal for the range which was also used to cook on.

It was not a very large flat with a living room, two bedrooms, and a very small area containing a cooker (behind which was a small coal storage area), a toilet with a very rickety door, and a bath, above which they had a hanging washing line on which they hung their washing. For a long time, they only had gas; electricity was finally put in after the war.

Just to explain, Fred's real name is Albert Frederick Brooks, the same as his Dad's, but he has always been called Fred by his family and Joe by his workmates. He nearly always refers to me as 'kid'.

My parents were very strict and if we wanted to go to the pictures or pantomime, I had to have special permission and Fred always saw that I got home on time. On Christmas Eve, when I was 20, I got engaged and we were very happy. Fred's sister Lily was lovely. She had heart trouble and she died before she was 21 and we missed her very much. Although her health was poor, she was a very happy person.

Ron: from information I have gleamed from Aunty Gladys, because Lily was not able to do much hard work due to her heart condition, she became a companion to Mrs Challicom, whose family owned the large furniture shop on the corner of Orchard Street and Denmark Street which is very close to where they lived. There is a lovely photograph of Lily sitting on impressive stairs in the building. Apparently, you entered the store from the front but walked down the side road and into an entrance there to get to the living accommodation. There is a large Challicom store in Clevedon to this day.

Mum: When my 21st birthday was near, Fred bought me a beautiful watch. He showed it to Lily and told her he would buy her one for her 21st birthday. She told him not to bother as she would not live that long. She died in the January just before her 21st and so Fred gave the watch to his mother.

It was a very sad funeral and Fred was so upset as he and Lily were so close and had plenty of fun.

Fred's mother went to South Wales for two weeks to stay with her sister Tam, but she was very unhappy and was pleased to come back home to all her family. She went back to her job working in the brewery. Fred's dad worked very hard and was so easy to get on with. He worked in a garage until he retired and then went to work part-time in the evenings in the Cathedral Garage on the Centre.

Fred's elder sister, Mary, was very nice, but was a proper 'Chapelgoer' and not as full of fun as Lily. She had epileptic fits and was on special medicine from London. Fred's mother was told that it would do Mary good, and it was quite expensive, however, after many bottles of it the fits went. Fred's youngest sister, Gladys, was about two years old when we started going out together. I got on well with Fred's mother initially, but when she realised we were going to get married and she would lose Fred's money, her attitude towards me changed completely as if to try to frighten me off. As an exact opposite to Fred's dad in many ways.

Ron: I believe that Mary belonged to the Plymouth Brethren. Some people called her 'Polly' but I did not know why. I later learnt that Polly can be a nickname for Mary.

Mum: We were married on July 20ᵗʰ, 1931, at St. Peter's Registry Office in High Street. My sister Flo gave me away as my dad could not take time off from work. Fred's Dad did not come to the wedding either. My Mum, Gran and many friends came to the wedding, but Fred's mum would not come and stayed home saying she had her washing to do. She did not want Fred to get married and when she knew we were going to do so, she offered to buy a house for us all to live together. Fred said no, and that we were going to live on our own. Fred's friend came as best man, and his girlfriend came as well.

We had a nice wedding meal in a restaurant on the City Centre, just Fred, me, Flo, and the best man and his girlfriend and it was the first time that I had tasted Champagne. It was lovely and so bubbly it made you laugh as you were drinking it. After our wedding meal we went to see Fred's mother. She was very quiet and not very sociable as she thought that Fred would never get married. We left to go to say goodbye to my Mum as we had to catch a coach from the Centre to get us to Birmingham.

Living in the same house as Fred's family in Pipe Lane, which they rented, was another couple called Mr (Billy) Buttons and his wife. They were very poor but very nice, and they gave us a beautiful cheese dish and teapot. Both were chipped but that did not matter as it was the thought that counted. (Ron: I still have both items in our house, and we treasure them. I have contemplated getting them repaired but somehow that would destroy the magic). We often had a laugh about Billy because he nearly always walked around with a row of medals on his chest. Fred asked him where he was stationed, and he told him that he had never been in the war!

My mum was so upset at me going to live so far away but Fred said we would come down every two weeks, which we did. The coach left Bristol at about 3.o'clock and we arrived at Birmingham about 9.30 p.m. It was a very hot day and plenty of sunshine.

Before we were married, Fred was moved to Birmingham by his company, Bristol Wireless. He was very happy in Birmingham and used to come home every Friday night and go back on Sunday, travelling through the night to start work on Monday morning. He managed to lodge with a very nice woman, and we continued to live there when we were first married. We had two rooms, a large living room, and a bedroom. We shared the kitchen with our landlady who had a young baby. Fred had ordered our furniture before the wedding, and the landlady arranged to be home when it arrived, so she made sure that the two rooms looked lovely for us. Her husband was also very nice, and we got on well together.

(Ron: Dad told me that when he was an apprentice electrician with Bristol Wireless one of his first jobs was to put up electric lights on Weston Pier to replace the old gas lamps).

Mum: Fred had two weeks' holiday and so that gave us a chance to see Birmingham. Fred went to work by car, his hours were 8.30 a.m. to 5. p.m., but sometimes he worked late. We often went to the pictures and the theatre; Birmingham was a very nice place to live. We first lived at Handsworth and stayed for about three months and then we were offered rooms at Hall Green. Birmingham has many beautiful canals you can walk alongside.

(Ron: I understand that there are more canals in Birmingham than in Venice!).

Mum: It was a lovely area to live in and plenty of shops to visit. The rooms in our new flat were much larger; we had our own kitchen but had to share the bathroom. We were very happy with Mr. and Mrs Anderson and their daughter. She kept a dress and wool shop and sometimes on a Wednesday I would look after the shop while she went to the warehouse to get more goods. Wednesday was usually a very quiet day.

Fred had the chance to buy a shop selling and repairing bicycles and we also had a petrol pump. We were doing very well but a friend of Fred's had petrol and did not pay regularly for it. He left Birmingham owing us a lot of money and because you had to pay cash every time you needed petrol, it left us in difficulties. We had to pay rent on our rooms as there was no living accommodation above the shop and so Fred decided to sell the business.

We stored our furniture in Birmingham and came back to Bristol to live. Fred stayed with his mother, and I went home to my Mum's as there was no spare bedroom available. I slept with my sister Flo and within two weeks we managed to get two nice rooms in Albert Park Place, City Road.

Mrs Pope and her husband lived there and another husband and wife with their four children. We had a nice living room and a large bedroom. To do my washing I had to go down to the basement and there was also a small garden, but I did not use it.

When we moved into our rooms, I knew I was pregnant. My mother used to go with me to the BRI for examinations and we were very happy to be expecting our first baby. Dorothy Lilian (her second name after Fred's sister) was born on the 13 January 1933. She was a beautiful baby and was 6½ lbs when born, but I could not feed her enough myself, so my mother put her on Nestles Milk and then, when she was about two months old, mum told me to give her Farley's Biscuits as milk was not enough.

Whilst I was expecting Dorothy, Mrs Buttons was expecting her third child – she already had two young ones. We went down to Fred's home in Pipe Lane to see his mother and the maternity nurse from the BRI was with Mrs. Buttons. It was a great laugh because Fred and his dad were betting with cigarettes what sex the baby would be. Fred won as it was a little girl.

My dad was so proud of his first grand-daughter and would take her out in her pram. Fred's mother came to tea with Mary every Monday. The rent man would call in the evening and Dorothy would cry and didn't want to go to Fred's mother. Fred worked so hard because wages were very small and then I realised that I was going to have another baby. (My Mother told me that she believed that women could not become pregnant whilst they were breast feeding). I was so worried, but my Mum said that I would manage, and she would help me in every way.

I booked to go into the BRI to have my baby. We bought a nice birthday cake for Dorothy's first birthday, but on that morning, I went into hospital and Florence (named after my sister) was born on Dorothy's birthday. My Mother looked after Dorothy and Fred went there every day to see her. My Mother was wonderful to us. When I came out of hospital Dorothy would not come to me and so she stayed with Mum who brought her every day to see me and her new baby sister. Dorothy did not want to stay with me; she wanted her Gran. Then one afternoon Mum left her hat and coat outside the door and then left quietly hoping Dorothy would not notice.

I could not stop Dorothy from crying and then Fred came home and held her and then let her hold her little sister. She settled down after a while, and when Mum came to see me, she never let Dorothy see her go. But the days went by, and I was able to go out. In those days, after you had a baby, you did not go out until you were 'churched' and the baby christened. Dorothy was christened at St. James Church.

I had a wonderful mother and father. They lived for a long time in a three-bedroom house in Holton Road, Horfield. After the war the government persuaded people living in large houses to move into smaller properties to make way for the many larger families who had lost their homes during the war. My mum used to take snuff which my dad hated and so she would buy it on her trips to the shops and hide it. Everyone knew what she was doing because her handkerchiefs were always stained with the stuff. She used to put a pinch of it on the back of her hand and sniff it, and then sneeze into them.

They were offered a brand-new prefab near Horfield Common at 32 Inkerman Close, Horfield, Bristol which was fully equipped with built in appliances. They also had a large garden and as my dad really enjoyed gardening, they accepted it. All their furniture etc was moved by a man with a horse and cart! The prefab had a beautiful garden that my father loved and worked hard in, growing vegetables and flowers. Dad worked very hard, and his last job was as a 'print feeder' at Nailsea Printing Works but he had a lot of travelling to work to do. He sometimes went by car (Ron: *he must have got a lift because I never saw him drive and they never owned a car)* and sometimes by bus as he worked different shifts. He would not work the night shift as Mum did not like being alone at night.

We would take Mum and Dad out for car trips which they really enjoyed. Dad retired from work at 65 because his health was not too good, he never really got over his treatment as a prisoner of war. He had 'water trouble' and had to have an operation at Frenchay hospital. We were going on holiday that weekend and Dad told us to carry on and go. We came home on the Saturday and went straight to see Dad. He was much better and came home the following week. He was still so poorly at times that Mum eventually sent for the Doctor, and he was admitted to Southmead Hospital at the same time as my daughter Flo was ill in the BRI.

My Dad became very ill and died in Southmead Hospital on Christmas Day 1965 aged 76. Flo had two children, Carol, and Philip and so Fred and I looked after them. When we visited Flo and my dad, Ron, and Jean (*who lived close by in Coronation Road*) looked after them. Flo was in hospital over Christmas, and we went to visit her on Christmas afternoon and then went on to visit my Dad.

I kissed my Dad on the cheek but got no response from him. Fred looked at him and went straight to find a nurse. When she came, she told us that Dad had passed away. It was a terrible shock and we had to go over to Pearl and Stan's where my Mum was staying. I will never forget how shocked Mum was.

(*Ron: This is a day I remember well and with great sadness. We were living in Coronation Road, Ashton, Bristol, and had invited Mum and Dad to tea but they were delayed at the hospital. I was putting Beverly, who was three years old, to bed as I always did. She slept in the middle bedroom of the house – she liked her bottle of Ovaltine at that time, and I would stay with her whilst she drank it. And then she would fall quickly to sleep. I heard Jean answer the front door and then my Mum say 'My Dad's dead. She was totally devastated, and Christmas was never the same again*).

Mum: Mum was very lonely but went back to her prefab in Horfield. We all visited her. I worked from 8.00 to 2 o'clock at Robinsons Bag makers in Argus Road and we would visit Mum every Wednesday and Saturday. She really looked forward to our visits. She was very fond of Fred and would always listen to his advice.

They had some lovely neighbours in Mrs. Corrie and Mrs Bohan, and they used to have a good laugh together in the garden. Mrs Corrie and her husband did not go out much as his health was not good and my Dad would go over to have a talk with him when he was too poorly to go outside. He died very suddenly, and Mrs Corrie was very lonely. Sometimes when Mum went shopping, she would walk up the road with her.

Mum used to have a bath on Saturday mornings and change her clothes as she always liked to go out clean. She said that if she was taken ill she wouldn't like not to be clean. We would take her to Weston and Clevedon and other rides and would have a meal of fish and chips. She was a very slow eater, and she would worry if the shop was packed so she asked us if we could eat the fish and chips at home. We would get her home by 7.30 p.m. and Fred would go to the fish and chip shop and get our supper. I would make tea and we would sit and enjoy our meal. We would leave her about 9.30 p.m., and she was so pleased to spend the time with us.

My brother Bill and his wife Doreen would also have her to tea some Sundays and would also take her out for rides. My sister Flo and I kept Mum's home clean; Flo did the washing, and I did most of the cleaning, but we cleaned the windows between us. Mum was a wonderful mother and no trouble to any of us. After that my mother would go to stay with my brother Stan and his wife Pearl at week-ends and after she was found wandering about the garden with no clothes on in the early hours of the morning, she went to stay with them and gave up her prefab.

This did not work out as in her prefab she was on the ground floor but at Stan's she had to go upstairs to bed. I think that is why one day she said to Fred and me that she would like to go into St. Joseph's Home. Mum was a Catholic, and so Fred, Stanley my brother and myself went to see the Mother Superior. Knowing that mum could help herself they admitted her to the Home, and she moved there in the October. She was deeply upset when we left her there; she wanted to go back home to her prefab.

After a few days she settled down and was happy there. Her birthday was on the 5th December and so Fred ordered a nice birthday cake and some flowers, and the Sisters of Mercy (nuns) invited us all to tea. We had a lovely time, and the birthday cake was shared among the patients. I would visit her every Wednesday and Fred and I would go in every Sunday. My brothers and sisters would cover the other days.

She started to get very feeble and eventually could not get out of bed. She died on 3rd November 1977 and would have been 90 on the 5th December 1977. The funeral was from St. Joseph's home, and they gave her a wonderful service and all the patients who could walk or be wheeled there attended.

Mum was buried in the same grave as my dad, in the Catholic Cemetery at Arnos Vale, Brislington, Bristol. Mum did not like cremations and was happy to know that we would bury her. We had a nice headstone put there and we visit the grave frequently as we miss her very much. She was no trouble to any of us.

While Mum was in St Joseph's Home my brother Stanley was taken very ill and had to go into hospital. He came out of hospital but shortly afterwards Mum died, and he was able to go to the funeral. We all went back to my sister Flo's house after the funeral. Stanley became very ill again and went into Frenchay Hospital where he died from cancer in May 1978. Mum never knew about this, and we were pleased that she died first as she loved all of us, but Stan was her youngest son and the only Catholic and she loved him dearly,

Before we lived in Southmead we lived near Gloucester Road. Fred was very friendly with a Mr. Gibson who lived in Summerville Road, off Gloucester Road. He had a large house and lived alone. He asked Fred if we would like to go and live with him. We had a nice living room, two bedrooms, and a kitchen and we shared the bathroom. I used to clean his rooms and keep the garden tidy and so he gave me a small wage, which was a great help. Summerville Road is near St. Andrew's Park, and I used to go shopping and come back through the park. The summers used to be very hot, and we would spend evenings in the garden.

Before we left Albert Park, we had Flo christened at St. Barnabas Church in Ashley Road. She was about two months old when we went to live with Mr. Gibson, and we stayed with him for about two years. Then in 1936 Mr. Gibson had to renew the lease of his house, but the owner told him he was too old to renew the lease as he was about 60 years old.

We already had our name down for a council house and so Fred went to the Council, and they gave us a nice house at 17, Coleford Road, Southmead, which we really loved.

It had a large kitchen with a huge dresser in it, a front room, three bedrooms and a bathroom upstairs and a nice garden. The toilet was immediately outside the back door, and, whilst it was undercover, it was very cold in there in the winter and scary in the dark. Spiders could also scare the living daylights out of you!

You never liked being caught in there when someone knocked on the back door, I don't know why but you felt awkward coming out of the lavatory (as it was called then) or calling out to them to hang on. The toilet paper was squares of newspaper, skewered, string put through the top corner, and the pack hung on a nail. This is where news was often read, and it was often frustrating when you could not find the bit that continued the story.

In the kitchen was a large gas boiler which was used for many purposes. When the water was hot enough it could be pumped by a hand pump, which was on the wall right next to the boiler, up to the bath which was in the bathroom immediately above. The boiler was also used to boil up the washing into which I use to put a bluey bag to keep clothes white. A boiler stick was used to move the washing around in the boiler and to threaten (but never used) the children with if they were naughty. At Christmas times I always boiled the Christmas puddings for hours and they were loved by everyone.

Outside at the back of the house we had a huge mangle which would squeeze most of the water from the clothes which were then hung on the clothesline and pushed up as high as possible with the prop to dry in the wind. This was very hard work and bitterly cold in the winter as the clothes had to be rinsed in cold water. People took great pride in their washing, and you were judged on its white-ness. There was also a strict order for hanging things up – all of this you were taught by your mother.

We also had a gas cooker that we had bought from the gas board on the 'never-never'. It was guaranteed for life, and we paid for it quarterly. When Fred was called up for the forces, I found it very difficult to pay for and then the gasman told me that all payments for servicemen had been suspended until after the war, it was such a relief.

I had a very big scare not long after we moved to Coleford Road. I was in the front garden when a lady came to the gate and said that Fred had been knocked off his bike on Southmead Road and she thought he was dead. I ran up the road feeling shocked and terrified, but luckily he was not badly hurt, just shook up.

We made friends with Mr. and Mr Smith (Ernest and Edith) who had three boys Kenneth, Walter 'Wally' and Mervyn and a girl (Joan) and our children were very hap-py together. I had stomach trouble and had to go into the BRI for about four weeks. She was a wonderful friend and helped look after the two girls while Fred was at work.

Then in 1938 I found out I was pregnant, and Edie told me not to go into hospital as she would look after me and my family. My son Ronald was born on the 14th of November 1938. He was a lovely baby with auburn hair, and we were so pleased to have a son. We had lots of fun and happiness especially on Bank Holiday weekends when we would all go across the fields and take a picnic lunch. Fred and Ern Smith would lift Ron in his pram over a hedge as there was not a large enough gap to push a pram through. We often went to Canford Park, in Westbury on Trym where they had children's swings, roundabouts and a very large fishpond. The children had a wonderful time.

Dorothy and Joan Smith went to Fonthill Road School and Flo went to Doncaster Road School. Flo came home from school and said her teacher, Miss Rowbottom, wanted to see the new baby sometime. Fred used to torment Flo and say 'did you take the baby up to see Miss Blackbottom? Flo would get very upset and would say 'It's not Miss Blackbottom, it is Miss Rowbottom'. I took Ronald up to see her teacher and Flo was delighted and pushed the pram all the way home.

(Ron: I do not know whether Mum mentions this later, but Dad was very keen on all things mechanical. In the back garden apparently, he had an old motorcycle and one day a 'rag and bone man' came to the door and asked if he could buy the motorcycle for a very good amount. Mum thought this was too good to be missed and agreed. The man said that he did not have sufficient money but would take the bike away and return the same evening with the cash. Mum was very pleased about this (and very naïve) and told Dad about it when he got home from work. Dad rightly guessed that the man would never return with the money – and he was right.)

Mum: In 1939 the Second World War broke out, it was terrible. Fred had to go into the forces in December 1940. He joined the Royal Air Force as a driver and for a time he was stationed just outside of Bristol which meant he managed to get home some weekends. Mr Smith was also called up and joined the army and for a long time was stationed in Exeter, close enough for him to come home most weekends or for Mrs Smith to visit him.

When Fred came home on leave Ronald was so pleased to see his dad who was wonderful with all the children. We all dreaded him going back off leave and Ron used to sit on the sewing machine in the window. Fred told him he was going up the road to the shops and would not be long. Ron would sit there waiting for Daddy to come back. He would cry so much that it was really upsetting for him and me. When Fred went abroad, he settled down to not seeing Daddy.

Peter was born on 13th April 1941 and Mrs. Smith and my sister Violet were with me at my confinement. Mrs Smith phoned Fred and he was given compassionate leave as I had a very bad confinement. I was told that I was not to have any more children.

(Ron: my very first memory is that of Aunty Vi taking me downstairs to see my new brother. I can remember the bed being on the wall opposite the window which had crosses of brown tape across each small pane to stop the glass from shattering into the room – 1941 was a very bad year for bombing and we lived only about four miles from the BAC in Filton which was heavily bombed with lots of casualties) In later years Vi was able to confirm my memories for me.

Mum: After Fred's compassionate leave he went back and was sent abroad with the Royal Air Force attached to the

Eighth Army. My brother Bill was also in The Royal Air Force, and they managed to meet up once while they were abroad, which was lovely. Fred was away for a long time and mail was not reliable. When he received my letters, and I received his (they tended to come in batches) we had to sort out the dates first and then read them in date order. Fred said it was like reading a book.

(Ron: My memory of Dad going away was in our front room and me being held in Mum's arms and her saying that Daddy would be away for some time. He then left going out the front door (which we did not normally use). Every Sunday Mum would make all of us children stand on the sideboard and kiss Dad's photograph which was of him in his Royal Air Force uniform. This was so that we would not forget him.

Mum: We had to have black-out at all the windows, and they built air raid shelters in the gardens. We had an 'above ground' one but we never used it. We also stuck brown paper tape in an X across the panes of glass to stop them from splintering from bomb blasts. The first air raid warning came one Sunday morning, and I pushed the three children under the kitchen table. I was making toffee apples at the time and so the children were quite happy underneath there. It was a false alarm, but London had received air raids, so it was a proper warning to us.

When the first air raid came there was no siren warning to let us know what was happening. Dorothy and Flo had gone to school and Ron was indoors playing with his toys. I went into the garden and was talking to my neighbour, Mrs Marshall, when a lot of planes flew overhead.

We thought they were English, but they flew over Filton aerodrome and started the bombing raid. It was a terrible raid with so many killed in the shelters. I rushed indoors and put my son under the table and stayed there until the planes flew away and the 'all-clear' was sounded.

I put Ron in the pram and went to meet Flo and then on to meet Dorothy and Joan Smith, but they were both nearly home by the time I met them. It was a great relief to know that they were safe. After having that first raid we were always on the alert, and as soon as the siren sounded, we went over to Mrs Smith's shelter as there was room for all the children to lie down and sleep while Mrs Smith and I used to stay outside of the shelter talking to the wardens for as long as it was safe. I was expecting Peter and had to lay under the bed until the all-clear sounded, which we all did whenever we could not get across to the shelter.

The air raids grew worse and during one air raid the children were playing next door in Mrs Marshall's, and I rushed to put them into the Anderson Shelter in her garden (half below ground, half above ground and covered with soil and grass). Mrs Marshall was having a bath and she came racing out of the house wrapped only in a bath towel. We had a good laugh about it, but it could have been very serious.

(Ron: I remember waking up one morning and coming downstairs to find that the ceiling in the front room (we did not call it a lounge in those days) had come down during an air raid and there was filthy mess everywhere. People came to

help Mum clear it up and then workmen came to repair the ceiling, but we were many days with sheets covering the furniture. My Dad also told me that during one raid whilst he was at home, he opened the front door slightly to see what was going on, only to be thrown back across the hallway and onto the stairs by a bomb blast that almost took the front door off its hinges.)

Mum: When the war started, we were put on rations and we each had a ration book and were allowed a certain amount of food each week. I was able to let Mum have some of our rations such as tea etc because we had a book for each child, and they had only two books. Mum was very pleased that I could help. Dorothy and Flo would come up to Mum's straight from school and have tea. Mum had an air raid shelter in her garden at Holton Road, Horfield, but did not like going into it unless someone was with her.

I often laugh when people speak about having their chimneys swept. You had to have your chimney swept regularly otherwise the soot trapped up there caught fire and could be very dangerous. Some people let this happen rather than pay to have it swept in any case. If the fire brigade came out, or if a policeman arrived before the flames went out you could be fined, and Fred and I never took that chance. It was quite spectacular watching the flames come out of the chimney pot but could be a real hazard.

Mrs Smith ordered the sweep one Saturday morning and prepared her room, covering everything over with cloths.

The siren went at 9.00 p.m., and we were in the shelter all night and until about 5 o'clock in the morning, when the bombing ended and the 'all clear' was sounded. When we went back into Mrs Smith's front room all the soot had come down the chimney and covered everything. Her carpet was the only thing not covered and was ruined and Edie (Mrs Smith) had to eventually buy another one: not easy in wartime!

Mrs Smith would go out working every day and she rode a bicycle which she enjoyed doing. Her legs were very bad as she had varicose veins, but she would not go by bus. When she got home from work which was usually about 3.00 p.m., she would either come over to me or I would go to her house for a cup of tea.

Mrs Smith was very strict with her children and if they were naughty, she would hit them with a large wooden spoon. It was a proper joke with my daughters. I was strict with my children, but rarely did they get a smack (*although she would threaten us with the boiler stick!*) The children are still friendly with the Smiths to this day.

Fred went abroad by boat and was in Sardinia and many foreign towns. He was in the desert and in South Africa. He then flew back to France where he was stationed for some time towards the end of the war.

(*Ron: One of the mysteries that I need to solve is how Dad came to be so badly burnt during the war. When he came home from the war, the back of his neck was very red and swollen and looked like orange peel. He would not say too much about it and then, in about 1946 he and Mum took me and Peter to visit a family in Sea Mills in Bristol. The lady made Peter and I some chips which we ate in the kitchen whilst they all went into the front room where they were talking very quietly, and it was obviously a very sad occasion because we could hear sobbing. In later years a few more details came out and Dad was the sole survivor of a tent fire in the desert.)*

To keep out insects they dug a trench around their tent and filled it with petrol – a dangerous and stupid thing to do. When the tent went up in flames Dad was standing in the entrance looking out. He was the only one to get out, badly burnt, whilst the others all died (I believe it was three dead, but I have heard different numbers quoted). There was a court of inquiry, but Dad could not admit to what had happened or who was to blame otherwise if found guilty of illegal activities the relatives of the deceased would get no compensation.

I am convinced that we went to visit a relative of one of the deceased. I must see if I can access the notes of the Courts of Inquiry when I have time available.

Mum: During the war many of my neighbours had to go to work but, as I had four children to look after I did not have to. When our rent was due, I would pay about eight neighbours' rent. The rent man would call, and he would have a cup of tea as my house was his last call. I used to get very worried sometimes having eight rents to pay especially when we had air-raids. But everything turned out OK and I made some wonderful friends and neighbours. After we moved to Smyth Road, I would visit Mrs Smith and I nearly always met some friends, and we would have a good laugh and talk about old times (and sometimes some tears).

Whilst Fred was abroad with the Royal Air Force his mother was taken ill with influenza and was poorly for some time. One day when I went to visit her, she could not see very well so I asked her to see a doctor. She was very stubborn and would not go to see one or call one out. I advised her to have her eyes tested and I went with her to Hyde Baines the optician in High Street. She had glasses but didn't like wearing them.

Gladys was working in Frenchay Hospital at the time as a nurse, but she had to stay at home to help her mother. Mary, Fred's other sister worked at Maggs Furnishing Department. She used to go to people's homes to repair sofas and to put new furnishings on chair seats but her main job during the war was to go to Avonmouth Docks to put new furnishing on the ships and carry out repairs. This was work governed by the tides and so she was away a lot overnight.

Eventually the air raids eased off, but we had to be on the alert. Time passed and I used to take Ron to school because the girls were old enough to go on their own. I had a very dear friend Mrs Robbins who lived in Wilton Close. She had three children and before Peter started school she would come up and have a cup of tea. Perhaps we would go for a walk together, but we always got back home in time for the children coming home from school.

One very hot day Mrs Robbins came to see me, it was too hot to go walking and so Peter and Hazel played in the garden, and we gave them lemonade and biscuits and we had our cups of tea. When we went to bring them in the gate was locked but they were not in the garden. I went one way and Mrs Robbins went the other way. When I got to Charfield Road I met some neighbours who said they had seen them both in Fonthill Road. I ran and met them and took them home where they both got a smack.

Mrs Robbins and I could not understand how they got out and so the next day we gave them lemonade and biscuits in the garden again and we watched from the window to see what they would do. They both went to the hedge and crawled through the gap in the bottom. We flew out the door and soon had them back indoors. They never went out of the garden again.

Mrs Darby, who lived opposite us had five children and was expecting another baby. Her husband was in the army at the time but even when he was home he was totally unreliable. She said her sister (Grace) was going to be with her at the confinement, but before I tell you anymore, we had a lot of Irish people come to live at Southmead. We were asked to take these Irish men in as lodgers, but I said no. Mrs Darby had an Irish lodger, but I had not met him.

She was in labour and her neighbour, Mrs Goering, (who used to go out with Mrs Darby a lot), was staying the night with her. At about 2 o'clock in the early hours of the morning her labour pains started, and Mrs Goering came over to tell me what was happening. My four children were asleep, so I went over to see her. I didn't know that they had got in touch with the hospital already. I was getting worried as no nurse had arrived and I was in the room by myself. There was only this man sat by the fire reading a book and I thought he must be the Irish lodger, and so I asked him to leave the room.

He said 'I'm used to this' and went on reading. A knock came on the front door and when I answered it, I recognised the Sister who was with me when Peter was born. She was pleased to see me. When she entered the room, as the bed was downstairs, she said, 'Oh you have arrived then'. I went into the kitchen where Mrs Goering was having a doze and asked her who the man was. He was the doctor who had come for the confinement. I went back in and apologised to him, the Sister was helpless with laughter, and he was very nice! We had a good laugh. He thought I knew that he was the doctor.

Mrs Darby's sister, Grace, arrived and so I left her to look after her sister as I had four children asleep at home. Grace continued to look after her sister until after the baby was born. A couple of months later, Frank, Mrs Darby's eldest son, came across, and told me his mother wanted to see me. When I went over she was passing blood and so I went up to the telephone box and asked for the doctor to come.

My doctor turned up and I showed him what she had passed, and she was taken to the General Hospital. After a few days Grace met me at the hospital and told me the bad news that Mrs Darby had cancer. She said she could not bear to tell Mr Darby and so I went home and discussed it with Edie.

We asked Mr Darby, who was home on leave, to come across and we broke the news to him. She was allowed home from hospital, and Edie and I to look after her, making different types of dishes to help her appetite. Fred said he would not allow me to do the washing as she had two able bodied sisters and they had to help look after her and her family.

Whilst we lived in Coleford Road (No 17) our next-door neighbours (No 19) were Mr and Mrs. Marshall with their two sons and three daughters. There was Gerald, the eldest, Olive and June (the twins), Joy and Donald. We had good times with her children going to school with my daughters. Gerald went abroad to Australia when he was about 16, but he did not keep in touch, and they were very worried about him. They got in touch with the Red Cross, but they could not trace him. Mr and Mrs Marshall were very distressed, but the years passed by, and they never heard from him and there was a suspicion that he had been killed.

Their eldest daughter, Olive, gave birth to a baby when she was about 17 years old. She wasn't married and sadly her baby died. She took the baby in a small white coffin on her lap to Canford Cemetery where it was buried. It was most upsetting, and they were very upset. In those days it was terrible for a person to get pregnant and not be married, but the loss of a baby is very distressing.

Dorothy and Flo used to go to the church clubs with Olive, Joy and June and they often used to come in for supper after they got home at about 9.00 p.m. Mrs Marshall was amazed at this as her children never got anything to eat after teatime. My children were only given hot cocoa and biscuits, but they really enjoyed it. Ron and Peter were very friendly with their other son, Donald, but he was quite ill for a lot of the time and confined to his bedroom. He eventually recovered and trained as a barber at Max's on Southmead Road and won several hair styling competitions.

Mr Marshall was very nice, and he worked as a chauffeur to a very nice family who lived in Clifton. He was very friendly. I loved singing and he used to sit on his back step listening to me. I didn't know he was listening until he asked me why I hadn't sung that morning. I used to sing quite a lot, I loved singing and was in the Sunday Evening Choir at City Road and later the Southmead Baptist Choir. Mr Marshall died suddenly, and Mrs Marshall stayed on her own for many years. All the children got married and sadly she complained that they did very little for her.

I must admit that she was hard to get on with at times, but we were very good neighbours and during the war she would pop in to see me. She was very frightened of the air raids, but I could not share her air raid shelter as it was not large enough. It was an 'Anderson' shelter, half underground with corrugated sheets on the top that were covered in soil and grass.

Ron: Mrs Marshall had a very sharp tongue and I fell foul of it on a couple of occasions. The first was on a very hot day when I was about five. Earlier in the week we had been watching a fire drill being carried out by the Air Raid Precaution (ARP) members and they had used a stirrup pump to simulate how to put out a fire.

Everyone was told to stay indoors and so we were watching from our bedroom window as it was to take place on Mrs Organ's house, who lived almost directly opposite. Her husband was in the ARP, but I do not know why he was not in the services like the rest of the men. At the allotted time the team came running down the road with a ladder and some stirrup pumps.

They then tried to put out an imaginary fire, but the water would go up only just above the downstairs windows. Mum and Mrs Smith thought this was hilarious. Later I was playing in Mrs Marshall's garden with Donald. His dad, who was also not in the services, had a stirrup pump shut in the air raid shelter. Donald decided to play with this, and we put the bottom in a bucket of water and squirted it everywhere. We both got absolutely soaked and Mrs Marshall was horrified and gave us a good telling off.

She then took both of us into our house and told Mum how annoyed she was with us. Mum said that it was just water, and no harm was done as we were only having fun. Mrs Marshall stormed off in a huff. The next time was just after the war. Donald was very good at darts, and he had won a set of darts at the local fair. He said he would try to win a set for me, and Mum gave him three pence to try. You were given three darts to throw at a board with playing cards stuck on. If you managed to put all three darts into three cards you won a prize. Donald was successful again and I had my first ever set of darts.

We made a dartboard by drawing it on some old timber and had many hours of fun. At Christmas Mum and Dad bought me a proper dartboard and let it slip that Mrs Marshall had also bought one for Donald. I went in to see Donald later in the morning and told him that I also had a dartboard. Mrs Marshall was furious. Apparently, they did not open their presents until after lunch and she told me off and said I had spoilt his surprise.

Mum and Dad had always put our presents at the bottom of their bed and as soon as they were ready to get up, we were always allowed to go in to see what we had. We were always awake long before they were ready, and it was agony waiting. I could not believe that he would be made to wait until the afternoon. But that is what we do now, and that is because we travel to other peoples' houses on Christmas Day and open our presents there.

Dad put the dartboard up in the front room on the door leading out to the front porch. We had a great many hours of enjoyment, but the door ended up looking as if it had woodworm even though Dad had tried to protect it with a timber surround.

Mum: When Ronald started school at Doncaster Road, I would take him at first, and then he was able to go on his own with his friends. He was so late sometimes in coming home from school in the afternoon that I asked him why it was. He said he had been up the Greenway farm to see his pony. I thought that I had better follow him to see where he was going. I waited a short distance away and he went up the road to Greenway Farm which was at the top of Doncaster Road before they built Greystoke Avenue. I went home and later he turned up as well. I asked him where he had been and he told me, and so I said that the next day I would meet him from school, and he could take me to see the pony.

The farmer was very nice and when the farm was compulsorily purchased by the Council, he said Ronald could have the pony if we had somewhere to keep it. I told the farmer that we only had a garden. Ronald cried so much when he couldn't have his pony, so I told him that if we had the pony in the garden the Council would make us leave the house as no large animals were allowed.

He settled down afterwards and stopped going to the farm so often, but still went to see his pony and on holiday time we would take the pony up some bread. The farmer gave Ron some rides on the pony, which made him happy, but he had to be home from the farm by 5 o'clock to have his tea with us. Sadly, the farm was compulsorily purchased to make way for Greystoke Avenue and the other new roads and new houses being built on the 'new estate' and we do not know what happened to the pony. From then on, as they built the 'new' estate', we were known as living on the 'old estate'.

As food was very scarce during the war the government asked everyone to 'Dig for Britain'. I put my name down for an allotment so that we could grow some of our own food. We were finally given an allotment in Lake Road, the site of two houses that had been completely destroyed in the air raids. Fred's sister, Mary, came to help me to dig it over. It was filled with large bricks and rubble and would have been a challenge for a man, let alone two women. Unfortunately, we had to give it up.

Towards the end of the war, Fred's mother was taken into the eye hospital for a few days. My friend, Mrs Robbins, Gladys, and I went to hospital by taxi. They kept her in and operated on her eyes. She was almost blind as they found she had glaucoma. Her eyes got worse, and she eventually went totally blind. For a while she went to the Blind school to pass the time and to do some work, but she did not like it and eventually gave up going. Florrie Watts lived on the floor below and would often go up to keep Mrs Brooks company. Florrie lived alone with her son Brian who was tragically killed when he was knocked off his bike near Temple Meads station.

(Ron: There were many frustrations during the war, and I remember the time that Mum and a load of other women got really upset. We had all walked to the Cabot cinema in Horfield (now demolished and turned into shops and student accommodation). I cannot remember the exact film, but we saw both 'King Kong' and the Wizard of Oz' about that time.

Much to Mum's annoyance the Manager would not let us in but made us queue for a very long time. Then a group of soldiers turned up escorting a group of Italian prisoners of war who were then escorted into the cinema before any of us. There was a lot of booing and annoyance that they were let in first when they could have let us go in ahead. I did not see Mum upset too many times, but this certainly did the trick!)

Mum: After the war I used to go to Fred's mother's house about three times a week, give her a good wash and do all the washing besides cooking her Sunday dinner every week. Mary was quite good but would rather go to chapel as often as possible. By then Gladys was married to John and was expecting their first baby (named Mary) and would only go in to help on a Saturday morning.

They had a 'home help' but she would only do what I call 'top and tail' Mrs Brooks and never bathed her. Mary got very poorly, and she had very bad rheumatism in her hands and feet so eventually I was bathing Mary once a week as well. It was very hard and difficult work getting them in and out of the bath safely. To give them all a break Gladys, John and Mary would book up for a fortnight's holiday and I would have Fred's mother at our house. We got on very well normally, but she was very domineering and often upset the peace in our home.

When Fred came home from the war in1946 he went back to work for Bristol City Council in Redcliffe Wharf as an electrician. He found it very difficult because he had to leave home at 6.30 a.m. to get the bus and during that period, we had some atrocious winters including the terrible winter of 1947 which went on for months. Everything was still on ration and coal was scarce and it was very difficult to get warm. *(Ron: I remember dad opening the front door from inside and calling us to show us that the snow was up to the letterbox).*

When victory was declared Flo painted a large V (about 18" high) with ... underneath in silver paint which did not amuse the rent collection man and stayed on the wall for a great many years.

(Ron: When the armistice was finally declared I remember everyone putting out their flags across the street from house to house and in their windows. We had a street party in Coleford Road (many such parties took place all around the UK) especially for us children. Tables were put along the middle of the road, and everyone helped to provide food as best they could as food was still on ration and very scarce).

When Dad and other servicemen came home, we had another street party which again I remember very well. The adults took part in such games as musical chairs and the adults also danced in the street. On the first bonfire night that Dad was home, the men built a huge bonfire in the middle of the street where Coleford Road meets Trowbridge Road. It was a huge blaze and a policeman turned up and told everyone to let the fire go out – but he added 'when I am looking the other way, I will not be able to see if you add anything else'. Where the fire had been, a large circle of tarmac had been burnt away and stayed like that until they did the road with tarmac and chippings.

In those days when they were doing road works there would be a 'night watchman' who would stay on site day and night, mainly to stop thieves from stealing the equipment. He would have a hut he could sit in and a brazier burning to keep him warm. We loved to stay out as late as our parents would allow, talking to him and listening to his stories.

Where pollution from the smoke fires was so bad it was always very smoggy in the evenings, and you could taste it. It was not until a lot of people were killed by the smog that the Government brought in the clean air zones and people had to burn smokeless fuel, but the situation did not really improve until the late 1960s.)

Mum: After working for Bristol Corporation for a few years Fred then managed to get a job as Manager of Eastville Electrics in Henleaze Road, which was owned by Mrs Malloy. As well as selling electrical goods he also did lots of repairs and it was while he was working there that he became friendly with a lady doctor who was eventually to save Flo's life after serious negligence by our own doctor.

It was much better for him travelling because he did not have to open the shop until 9.o'clock and could cycle there, but the shop stayed open until 6.00 p.m., so he was often late home. This was particularly annoying on a Saturday evening (it was a six-day week) because the whole family went to the Orpheus cinema on that evening and there was always a large queue to get in. He would often be late if he was kept back by a customer or doing some urgent work. We would get closer and closer to being allowed in and the tension would rise as we wondered if we would lose our place in the queue. He almost invariably made it, but often only by the skin of his teeth. The air was often frosty on such occasions, not only from me but also the children!

In 1946 Flo was taken ill and it became very serious. We were under Dr Taylor whose surgery was in Trowbridge Road and he was getting near to retirement. He did not seem to know what was wrong and Flo just got worse and worse and was confined to bed with the curtains drawn for most of the time. She kept asking for 'thin skinned oranges' which were difficult to come by and we all tried our hardest.

She got so bad that eventually Fred asked the lady doctor for help. She was very wary of doing this because of professional practices but, on the pretence of coming to pick up her iron that Fred was repairing, she was able to carry out an examination. She was appalled at what she found and immediately phoned for an ambulance and got her into Southmead Hospital within the hour. It was discovered that Flo needed an urgent operation as she had a mastoid that could have proven fatal.

It took a very long time for Flo to recover. When Fred came home from the war, we had a bit of savings, but this was all spent on medicine. Thankfully the National Health Service was introduced which meant that the rest of the treatment was free; it was wonderful. We could never thank Dr Leach enough.

While we lived at Southmead, we belonged to Southmead Baptist Church. The vicar was the Reverend F.T. Payne, and he was a lovely man. He fell in love and wanted to get married, which was forbidden in those days and so had to leave the church. It was such a shame as he was wonderful with the children, and it was a great loss. There was a plaque in the church put up after he died, and it was there until the church was demolished to make way for some houses.

I joined a Thursday evening meeting, and we had different demonstrations like cooking, dressmaking and electrical jobs. Fred would not go as he did not like clubs, but he was happy that I went.

Dorothy left school at 14 (the school leaving age then) and went to work at the Bristol Aircraft Corporation (BAC) in Filton where she trained to be a shorthand typist. In about 1948 she met a very nice young man named Bryan Greenhill. He worked for Dunn's the man's clothes shop in High Street. They started courting seriously and then he was called up for National Service and joined the army with the Glorious Glosters. He was very lucky because his regiment was split. Bryan was sent to Switzerland whilst the others were sent to Korea where a large number were slaughtered at the battle of Injun Hill, a famous battle.

Dorothy was married on 20 March 1955, and they propped Mrs Darby up in a chair by the window to see Dorothy leave the house in her bridal dress. She was a beautiful bride and MrsDarby said she did not want to miss seeing her in her bridal outfit. Dorothy and Bryan were married at Filton Church. It was a beautiful wedding, and we had the reception in a hall just along on the main road. They went on honeymoon and then came home to live in a nice flat in Horfield.

Although Flo was only one year younger than Dorothy, by the time she was14 they had raised the school leaving age to 15: she was not amused!. Flo went to work for Jolley's the department store at the bottom of Whiteladies Road. She did not stay there long and then went to work for Gibb's the Chemist in Portland Square. It was there that she met Dennis Porter (who she told me she liked straight away and was longing for him to ask her out), and quite quickly they started courting seriously.

Dennis was also called up for National Service and both lads were unlucky as, whilst they were serving, the government increased it from 18 months to two years. Dennis was posted to Catterick for most of the time, which was a very long way away and he was only able to get home on the odd occasions. However, in view of some of the dire postings to notorious trouble spots, he was fortunate to be in a safe place.

Mrs Darby got very much worse. I would make delicate dishes for her to eat, wash her, and go over late at night to see her settled down. Her sisters now visited her more often and did her washing and looked after the children. She died In June 1955 and was cremated at Canford Cemetery. Her ashes were scattered on the very peaceful piece of ground the crematorium had designated for such occasions.

Her family managed to get over her death eventually. She had a big family: twin daughters Grace and Margaret (one of them was later to commit suicide) Sheila and Rita and two sons Frank and Peter. They all finally got married and even Mr Darby married again.

I also had another dear friend, Mrs Lewis who was very house-proud. She worked at the University in Park Row, cooking and cleaning. Her husband and family were very nice, and we used to go to the club together on Thursday evenings. She was taken ill with cancer and died at home after a long illness.

One year later 26 March 1956, Flo and Dennis got married, again at Filton Church. It was another lovely wedding, and we had such a laugh. Some of Dennis's relations lived down in the country and they all came by coach. After the reception a lot of the family went by the same coach to the Temple Meads railway station to see them off on their honeymoon.

I did not go as a lot came back to our house in Coleford Road. We had a television, and it was the first time some had seen it. It was laughable to see the guests who had come back, sat on seats and on the floor and they couldn't take their eyes off the screen. It was so amusing to watch their faces, and when the other guests arrived back from the station our house was filled with laughter.

We had a wonderful time and many other lovely times when we lived in Coleford Road.

(Ron: I started work on 4⁴ October 1954 with the Port of Bristol Authority. I earned £3.17.6p (old money) a week and of that I had to give Mum and Dad £2 per week for bed and board. One of the first things they did with this extra money was to rent a television from Radio Rentals. It was only a black and white picture, and the screen was only about 12 inches across, but it changed our evenings forever. After we rented it we would sit in the darkened room with only a small light above the set. Our evenings of card playing, and other hobbies practically stopped from the night we first watched it.

Mum: While we lived at Southmead, Fred arranged a coach outing to see the Blackpool Illuminations organised by Mr Hemmings, a coach driver who lived in Charfield Road. So many friends wanted to go that we ended up with two coaches instead of one. We left Southmead on Friday evening and travelled all through the night arriving at about 7.00 a.m. on Saturday morning.

We had booked a nice hotel and had breakfast there about 8.30 a.m. Those who wanted could go to bed after travelling all night, but we all went out and headed for Blackpool Tower. We climbed to the very top of the Tower and had a beautiful view. Then we went back to the hotel for midday meal and afterwards we went to the carnival and all the side shows and entertainments which were wonderful. We then went back to the hotel for evening meal and then the coach arrived and took us to see the lights. We drove right up the main road under them, and it was a beautiful sight to see.

We then stopped and went into the Tower ballroom and watched the dancers. About 11.00 p.m. we all went into the fish and chip shop and had supper. Our friends let Fred pay and paid him afterwards. Fred said to the waitress "if we can't pay for our supper can we do the washing up?".

She was very hoity toity and said NO, we have a washing up machine. She could see the funny side of it afterwards, as we all started laughing and had a wonderful evening.

On Sunday morning we had our breakfast and then went to Blackpool Tower for 'Community Singing' with some people dancing to the music. After that we went back to the hotel for our midday meal at 1.00 p.m. and then we left Blackpool and travelled home through the Mersey Tunnel which had just opened.

In 1957, when I was 48, I was taken to Southmead Hospital on the Wednesday as Christmas Day was on the weekend. I had a mastoid operation and was in hospital for two weeks. We had a lovely carol service on Christmas Eve with doctors and nurses going around to each ward singing Christmas carols. All the family came in on Christmas Day. I was moved from a side ward to be altogether in the big ward for the Christmas party. Father Christmas came round to each bed, and we all had a small Christmas present.

Doris Turner, a friend of mine was also in the same ward, she had 'head' trouble, and her mind was not too good, but she was feeling better and, although not perfect she left hospital. We had been friends for many years as we went to Day School and Sunday school and in the evenings to different clubs together. They had their own business, and her husband was the local chimney sweep.

Ron: I met Jeanette on Saturday 23 November 1957 at the Southmead Baptist youth club, and we started 'going out' together not long after. Dad, Peter, and I were useless at cooking because that was always 'women's work'. Jeanette stepped in and cooked Christmas lunch ready for us when we returned from hospital.

Dad was always a bit of a joker and he said to her (much to my embarrassment) 'If I placed two scolding hot pennies in

*your hand, what would you do. Jeanette replied, 'drop them'.
I was mortified when dad then said, 'what for two pennies?'
Luckily, she saw the funny side of it. She lived in the next road
to us and after I had walked her home my dad said to me: You
want to keep hold of that girl, she is attractive, can cook, and
has a good sense of humour. I took his advice!*

Mum: Fred's dad would frequently cycle from his home
to our house in Southmead. I will always remember him.
I used to do my baking on Saturday afternoons, and he
loved to come up and eat whatever I baked. He said to
me one Saturday that when Mother (his wife as he called
her) died he would come to live with me. I told him he
could not because he had Mary. He said that Mary could
look after herself.

Fred's dad retired from his job at Bryan Brothers when
he was 65 and then got an evening job with them from
5.30 p.m. to 10.30 p.m. He was a very good worker and
a good sport, and I was very fond of him. He came home
from work one Tuesday evening, had a cup of hot milk,
and then went to bed. Fred's mother went to get into bed
about half hour later and found he was dead. It was a ter-
rible shock to us all. When the police came to our house
to break the news to us, and said it was Fred's father, Fred
said 'No, you mean my mother is dead' as she had been
ill for years. My brother Stan was staying with us as his
wife, Pearl, was in hospital (she was expecting Lorraine),
so he went with Fred to see his mother and his dad's body.

It was a very sad time when he died because I really en-
joyed his company, and he was tremendous fun. The

Council decided to re-furbish St. George's House and so they moved Mrs Brooks and Mary from their top flat to a newly refurbished one. It only had one bedroom but a much bigger kitchen and bathroom. It was on the left-hand side of the buildings and this time on the second floor.

Because neither Mrs Brooks nor Mary could move very well they used to hang a key inside the door on a piece of string so that visitors could reach through the letterbox and get it to open the door from the outside. Someone got to know of this, or watched it happen, because one morning a young man opened the door and walked in and then, in front of them, stole their purses. It really shook them up and they were never able to leave the key like that again and Mary had to shout out frequently to let any visitor know that she was struggling to the door. They never caught the rat that did this, and I hope he rots in hell.

Mrs Brooks became more and more difficult to handle and so Gladys and I called the doctor who said that she would have to go to hospital. Fred was away that day repairing some radio sets. He often did this to earn extra money and would sometimes not get home until late. Mrs Brooks was told that she had to go to Manor Park Hospital, but she refused. (She would always say that the only way you came out of Manor Park was in a box!).

The doctor gave her an injection to sedate her and she was taken there by ambulance. She didn't realise for some time where she was until a friend who was visiting her told her. When Fred and I went in to see her she demanded to come home, but Fred told her that she was in the best place. Jean and Ron would take Mary to see her mother in hospital once a week, but they had to carry her down the stairs to the car and it got too much for them.

Fred used to talk and joke with other patients, and one time Fred's mother asked me where he was. I told her that he was talking to another patient. Although she was blind and couldn't see she looked straight at me and said that I wouldn't do a good turn for anyone. I asked her who had been looking after her before she was brought in here. When Fred came back, he asked me what was wrong, and I told him why I was upset. He was very annoyed, but I told him not to say anything to her; It was probably because of he drugs she was on. I did not go to see her on the following Sunday, but Fred went and told her she had a lot to thank me for.

She was in Manor Park for quite some time and then on 3 November 1975, we were all sent for, and she passed peacefully away. Fred was very upset, but I told him that we had done everything possible for her. She was buried at Avon View Cemetery in the family grave along with Lily and Mr. Brooks. We always kept the grave very nice.

After Fred's mother died, Mary continued to live in the flat in St. George's House, Hotwells. I often cooked for her, and I would take all her washing home and do it for her. Gladys visited her at weekends. It was pitiful to see her, and she could hardly move around, but Fred would not have her to live with us. She had many friends visiting her from the church and bringing her films that they could show her in which she was very interested.

For the first time in her life, she also had a television because Mrs Brooks would not allow one in the house while she was alive. I suppose that being blind it would not have been so good for her as the wireless was which she listened to constantly. We went to see her as usual one Wednesday evening in March and I gave her, her usual bath and she seemed better.

She was found dead by Gladys on the Saturday morning when she was on her usual visit. John, Gladys's husband, came over to our house to tell us and we went straight to the flat. The police was already there. The doctor came and it was about 5.30 p.m. before the undertakers came to move her body. I stayed in the kitchen as she was still sat in her chair where she died. The police said that only the undertakers would be allowed to move her.

We closed the flat and went to tell my mother what had happened as we were supposed to be taking her out for the afternoon. My Mum was very upset as she had known Mrs Brooks from their school days, and they were very friendly. Mum used to visit Fred's family now and again.

They had to have a post-mortem on Mary. It turned out that she had choked to death whilst, eating and had tried to use the telephone trying to call someone. Gladys and Fred went to get the death certificate from Moon Street mortuary. Mary was also buried at Avon View Cemetery in the family grave: the last of the four spaces.

We had to remove furniture from the flat quite quickly as it was council owned. We had a tea trolley and a clock, and the rest was given to family and friends. Gladys was also very upset, and we said that we would keep in touch as Fred was her only family left.

I worked for many years for Mrs Butler who lived at the 'Old Halt', a large house on the Downs. The family were very rich and owned the company William Butler and Sons which is a very well-known Bristol company producing and selling chemicals. I enjoyed my job and really loved it there. I worked Mondays, Wednesdays, and Friday mornings and another lady worked Tuesday, Thursday, and Saturday mornings.

Mrs Butler and her sister, Miss Cooper, were so lovely to work for. It was a large house but so easy to work. Miss Cooper died suddenly, and it was a great shock to us all. Mrs Butler was terribly upset. She was even sadder when her son, Peter, and his wife went to work away. I was with them for many years but had to give up working when I had my mastoid operation. Shortly afterwards Mr Butler died, and Mrs Butler was left on her own. I kept in touch and would regularly visit her for tea.

After a while she found that the 'Old Halt' was too big for her and so she sold it and went to live in a private nursing home in Bath. I continued to visit her about once a month, and she was so pleased to see me. Her health got very poor, and she didn't recognise people, and then her friend told me that she did not have long to live. I was very upset about it as she was such a wonderful lady.

She passed away and I lost touch with all the friends of hers who I knew.

In 1958 Mr and Mrs Smith's eldest son, Wally, had a terrible accident. He went on holiday with some mates to Jersey and they hired a car. One night they were returning to the hotel and the car crashed and overturned. Wally was asleep in the back when it happened, but he woke up just as the windows smashed and he was very badly injured. He was in hospital for a long time and lost the sight of one eye. Mr and Mrs Smith were devastated.

A policeman came and broke the news to them. We were the only people in the road to have a telephone (because of Fred being on call) and they used it every day to try to find out what was going on and they eventually were able to go to Jersey to see him in hospital. It took many years for Wally to recover and to come to terms with his disability as he had always been into all sports.

Fred worked for many years at Parker's Bakeries in Cotham. He was Assistant Chief Engineer under a man called Johnny Horner and he became Chief Engineer when Johnny retired. The General Manager (Mr Brown) was very nice, and his wife wanted a cleaner to help with the housework, so I went three mornings a week. She had two children and sometimes I would baby-sit for her to give them the chance to go to dinners given by the company. I worked for her for about three years but she added more work each week and so I went to work for Mrs Tebbs as Fred used to do all her electrical repairs for her.

Fred was offered a very good job at 'Associated Family Bakeries' in Smyth Road, Ashton, Bristol, as Chief Mechanical Engineer and it was a huge promotion. There had been a lot of problems at Parker's towards the end and Mr Brown had been removed and new management put in charge, and they wanted to put in their own people.

(Ron: While I was in the Royal Air Force, Mum and Dad let my room during the week to an engineer (Dave) who had come down 'so say' to understudy Dad and learn everything about the machinery. It turned out that he was there to replace Dad. Luckily Dad was offered the job with Associated Family Bakeries. He felt very bad about how he was treated and when he left they refused to pay him for hundreds of hours of overtime he had worked. He was particularly upset at Dave who it turned out knew all about the plans to replace Dad. Our family treated Dave very well and everyone thought he was nice, but it turned out otherwise.)

Mum: We had a car which he used for work, but it was a long journey from Southmead to Ashton. Sometimes he had just got home from work when he had to go all the way back for a breakdown in the machinery. Sometimes he had to crawl into the ovens to clear a blockage before they were properly cooled down as they had to keep production going and he would end up with burns and exhaustion.

He was offered the house next to the bakery (9 Smyth Road, Ashton) and we moved in December 1959. Living next door to the factory was even harder for him as he seemed to be on call all the time. He was always very tired, and I told him it was a pity we had moved there as we never seemed to have any family time and if we went out for the day he would be often called on. We lived there for about fifteen years.

(Ron: I was in the Royal Air Force, and they took me to see the house when I was home on leave for my 21st birthday. The new job offer was 'in the air' and they took me to Ashton to show me the house. They never actually told me the address as they drove me there but moved in not long afterwards. When I came home on leave the next time, which was for Christmas, I had to ask directions for the 'house next to the bakery!

Mum: I hated living at 9, Smyth Road. It was a very cold house with hardly any sunshine because we were right next to the large bakery. We had coal fires and had to burn coal, coke, chumps, (logs of wood) and we use paraffin stoves as well, just to keep the house warm; burning paraffin made the house run with water. The back garden was very small and dirty from the soot from the factory chimney and my washing was always getting speckled with dirt. We had a small front garden which I used to take care of as Fred did not like gardening and he would not have had the time even if he had liked it.

We had many shops in North Street and I would do a lot of my shopping in the 'Home and Colonial Stores'. One day Mr Porter, the Manager said he wanted a lady to do some morning cleaning and he asked me if I would like to try it. I went in at 8 a.m. until 1 p.m. mopping floors and cleaning counters. When we were very busy on Thursdays and Fridays, I would help to sort the customers' orders which Mr. Porter delivered himself.

He was very pleased with me, and I ended up most days serving the customers. However, he was taken ill and had to leave, and I did not stay long after that. Then I heard that they wanted kitchen help at Robinson's, the paper and bag firm.

Ronald (1949 to 1954) and Peter (1953 to 1958) both went to Cotham Grammar School, and both got good jobs when they left. Ronald went into the Royal Air Force to do his National Service on 4 February 1958. He had just started courting Jean (whose proper name was Jeanette). She is a very nice person and I liked her from the very first time I saw her. It was an anxious time because they were sending many young men to war, but we were very lucky, and he was posted to Chivenor in North Devon. Jean would visit us a lot while he was away, and we spent many evenings' together playing cards.

Her mother and father (Mr and Mrs Mallard) lived at 134 Charfield Road and I would sometimes go to see her mother and when she was going shopping, she had to pass my house and if the back door was open, she would call over the hedge 'put the kettle on, I won't be long' and then she would come in for a chat and a cup of tea.

Ron came home from the Royal air Force on 3 February 1960 and went back to his job with the Port of Bristol Authority at Avonmouth Docks in the office. Ron and Jean were married at Filton Parish Church on Easter

Saturday 1st April 1961. They were among the first couples to get married at the church because it had been closed for a while whilst they replaced the steeple (with a horrible small one!).

Fred, not long after coming out of hospital after losing one and a half fingers when the bread slicing machine blade jumped while it was being repaired. Health and Safety took back seat in those days and machines very often had no safety guards.

Peter was best man and they had two bridesmaids; Carol, (Flo and Den's daughter) was one and the other was the daughter of Jean's Aunty Gertie (Not sure whether it was Carol or Linda). There was a good turn-out and my Mum and Dad came along but could not go in for the service as my mum was Roman Catholic. Her great grandfather came from Rath Drum in Southern Ireland.

They had their reception in a church hall on Greystoke Avenue and there was a minor panic when we arrived from the church because the caterers had forgotten to bring any glasses, but they soon sorted it out and it was a lovely day. A big crowd went to see them off from Temple Meads station and they went to Teignmouth for their honeymoon.

About a month before the wedding Fred had a very bad accident when his hand was caught in the slicing machine whilst trying to repair it. He was rushed to the Bristol Royal Infirmary where he had an emergency operation. They came for me as we were living next door to the factory, and I went with him in the ambulance. It was the first time the ambulances had used the new siren, and Peter, who worked in Queen Square, heard the sound, and said to his mates 'some poor devil is in a hurry' not realising until afterwards that it was his dad.

Fred was in hospital about three weeks and then had to attend the outpatients department. He lost one finger completely, they had to remove it as it would have been permanently stiff and would have interfered with his job, and a half finger as well, both on his right hand. He always said for many years afterwards that the missing fingers caused him more pain than those which were left. It was touch and go whether he would be allowed to go to the wedding, but he made it, and you can see his hand all bound up and his arm in a sling in the wedding photo above.

Before the wedding Jean was living with her parents and Ron with us. They moved into a flat at 53 Ashley Road,

St. Paul's, Bristol together straight from their honeymoon and were very happy there. This left only Peter at home and the house seemed very lonely.

Things improved when Jean gave birth to Beverly on 14 June, 1962, and then in September they moved into a nice large house at 225, Coronation Road, Ashton Bristol. This was lovely because we were living within walking distance of each other, and I was able to help whenever needed. They had Joan (Jean's brother's girlfriend) who had come over from Ireland to stay with them for a time until she got her own place.

Peter was working for Bulmer's Cider in Queen Square, Bristol and in 1960 he met Maureen, who was working for Turner Edwards the shipping agents. They also had their head office in Queen Square. They met up during lunch times when a lot of office workers would take their sandwiches out and sit on the grass in Queen Square.

Peter got married to Maureen Wade on 7 September 1963 and Ron was their best man. At first they came to live with us in Smythe Road. We changed the small back bedroom into a kitchen so that they could be independent. Maureen's mum died and she was left some money and so they bought a house in Tennis Court Road, Kingswood, Bristol. I was left all on my own for the first time since Dorothy was born in 1933 and I did not like it one little bit.

Maureen and Peter have four children, two boys (Stephen and Andrew), and two girls (Karen and Sally Ann). After a while they bought a guest house in Ashcombe Road, Weston-super-Mare which they called 'Brooklans'. Maureen ran it whilst Peter went to work. By this time, he had become Transport Manager for Rank Xerox at Avonmouth.

Ron and Jean's son Martin was born at home in Coronation Road in the early hours of 7 May 1964. I stayed home from work for a few days to look after Jean and Martin, and Jean's mother would come over from Southmead as well.

It was lovely because I could walk to Coronation Road in five minutes, and we had a lovely time with the children playing in the garden. It helped me a lot because when we went to live at Smyth Road, I was very lonely, and I missed Mrs Smith, my friends, and my church.

I managed to get a job at a school on the Downs. It was a private school for boys, and it was owned by Mr and Mrs. Buckland. They were both very nice, Mr Buckland was the headmaster, and his wife helped him. They had two male teachers and one lady teacher, Mrs. Durie, who was also very nice. My hours were 9.00 a.m. to 2.00 p.m., and I used to get a bus there from Raleigh Road.

I worked in the kitchen preparing vegetables for the lady cook and after my job was done in the kitchen, I used to clean the drawing room and the private bedrooms. I was very happy there. Then the lady cook left, and Mrs Davies from Ashton came. Her name was Blod, and we got on very well together. Her husband would bring her over to my house at about 8.00 a.m. and we would go to work by bus together. We worked together for about three years and then she left and went as a cleaner nearer her home.

In about 1970, Mr and Mrs. Buckland sold the school and went to live at Crawley in Sussex. We still write to each other at Christmas and birthdays even after all these years (approximately 21). Blod Davies and I are still great friends and stay in touch. When I stopped working at the school, I got a job at Robinsons, the paper firm at Argus Road in Bedminster where I worked in the kitchen. My hours were 8.30 a.m. to 2.00 p.m., and we had a break of 15 minutes at 11 o'clock.

I worked in the canteen for about six and a half years with some very nice people serving meals and washing up. We used to prepare sandwiches for morning break at 10. o'clock and then Nancy, the head lady, would dish up the dinners and I would be on the urn serving cups of tea. I had another good friend, Flo, and we often went back to her house after work for a cup of tea.

It was a large canteen and the employees had excellent dinners and sweet afterwards quite cheaply. It was hard work, but I enjoyed it and made many friends.

One Saturday evening the company invited us to go to see a concert in Frogmore Street and have an evening meal. Quite a lot of workers went, and many remarked on how dirty the kitchens looked. The food (chicken etc.) was very greasy. On Sunday, the next day, I was very poorly but went to work as usual on the Monday morning. A lady came into the canteen and asked how many went to the Saturday night show and meal. All in our kitchen who went were poorly and we were all sent home because we had food poisoning.

All food we had prepared before the lady arrived which we had handled was thrown away. I was away from work with many of the other workers for two weeks and when we returned to work we had to wear rubber gloves. The restaurant was fined and closed for a period and lost a lot of customers.

We were a very happy crowd. There were two shifts, the other one was from 2 o'clock till 6 o'clock. The food was excellent, and we had a lot of fun together. You normally had to retire at 65 according to the rules, but I retired at 66. The head lady was very sorry to see me go as she didn't want to lose me. My friend Lyn retired at the same time and so the firm gave us a small party.

Our chef baked us a beautiful cake and we had sandwiches as well. They presented us each with a lovely bouquet of flowers. I had many presents and the chef made us both a small birthday cake and then they took us home by car. Nancy was very upset at our leaving and after I retired I used to go back to see her and other friends.

I also worked with a very nice person called Maisie. Her husband was a keen gardener, and she would bring in beautiful bunches of flowers, mainly dahlias and sell them to us. She sent my mother some and Mum said that she had never seen flowers so large. Her husband died suddenly but she had a wonderful family and they looked after her well.

She was a large built person but full of fun. She was very fond of Fred, and they always had a good laugh together. I was still so lonely and missing my friends from Southmead. I had the afternoons free and every Wednesday after work I would visit my mother in Horfield and Fred would come to pick me up in the evening.

(Ron: I know that Mum loved her mother, but she worshipped her father who had the most amazing sparkling and twinkling blue eyes. Every Wednesday without fail she baked him a cake and took it up with her).

Mum: My daughter Flo had a small dog called 'Timmy' which we would look after when they went away on holiday. As soon as I got home from work, he would look at his lead and I would take him for a walk to Ashton Park. He was good company and I remember on one occasion I wanted to find the street where Blod lived as I had promised to visit her.

I walked a long way, not realising that I would have to walk all the way back as I had forgotten to take my purse for bus fare. I didn't even find the road Blod lived in. When we got home Timmy, with his tiny legs, was exhausted. He drank a full dish of water, and then slept for about four hours. I was really worried about him but when he woke up he was fine and full of fun.

Every year the company gave us a dinner at the Grand Hotel in High Street, Bristol. I only went twice as I didn't like leaving Fred by himself. He would take me and pick me up after the party, which started at 7.30 p.m. until midnight, so it was very late. They did have a coach that picked people up, but it would be about 2.00 a.m. in the morning before I got home by the time they delivered others to their homes.

Robinsons gave all the pensioners a Christmas party at the works canteen during the first week in December, My friend Bertha used to take me by car. It started at 2.00 p.m. and went on until about 5 o'clock. Bertha's husband would be waiting outside to take us home and he would also give Maisie a lift. It was lovely to see old friends again. We had a nice Christmas Tea and then the Head Person would tell us how the firm was getting on.

At first they also used to give us £2 and a calendar, but then the firm was not doing so well so and so then they only gave a calendar. Last November they wrote to everyone saying that because of their poor trading situation, all Christmas parties were cancelled. It did not matter, really, because I have not been for the last two years owing to my illness.

Fred also had to retire when he was 65. We were still living in the house in Smythe Road that belonged to the bakery. Even though we had lived there for 16 years, we had to move out. We knew this would happen and so had put our name down for a Council flat. The company sent a letter to the Council telling them that we had to leave the house because it was 'Tied accommodation'. We were offered this flat on the fifth floor of Waldergrave House in Hartcliffe, and we have been here ever since. I love my flat; I have a wonderful view from the fifth floor and many friends.

The lady we took the flat over from told us that if we were as happy as she was in the flat, we would never leave it. She had to go to live with her daughter in Bedminster Down owing to her health and her age (70).

Fred managed to get a part time job at Luton's Bakery from 8.30 a.m. to 2.00 p.m. and he went round rewiring all their shops. Fred carried on his part time work after I retired. I was so happy in my flat and we had such a lovely outlook. Then Fred had a slight stroke and so he had to give up his part time job. We were both on a pension and managed quite well.

Ron: Although Mum called it a slight stroke it was in fact quite serious, and he never really got over it. His mouth continued to sag slightly even after he was much improved and, particularly when he was tired. I visited him the moment I heard from Dorothy about it, and when I got there, he was very frightened and broke down in tears.

He was terrified that he would not recover, and it took some time for him to do so. I visited him as often as I could, and it transpired that he was quite bitter, and blamed it on all the rushing around that Mum wanted to do in looking after her Mother, and her family. They were both very independent people and as I was the eldest boy they had a very strict talk to me.

They had seen how relatives moving in with you could destroy all your lives. It was their wish to live independent lives for as long as possible. That was their wish and one I was able to ensure that happened.

Mum: After his health improved, Fred started driving his car again. He was an excellent driver, but I got very nervous as sometimes as his right arm would go limp. So, we discussed it and I said to him that he was a careful driver, but it was other people speeding that could cause an accident. He was very upset at having to sell his beloved Volvo, but we had some wonderful times going by bus, and all the family helped us when we had anywhere special to go.

In 1976 my mother wanted to go into St. Joseph's home in Clifton. Mother was a Catholic and my Dad was a Protestant. We children were all brought up in Dad's religion except Stanley, my youngest brother. My Mum really wanted all of us to be Catholics, but my Dad would have none of this until Stanley was born and he relented. Stan had to go to a Catholic school in Trenchard Street.

When Stan was in the army, he was courting a girl called Audrey, but she jilted him and went off with a fireman called Dave who she subsequently married. Stanley was devastated at first but then he courted one of Audrey's friends, Pearl. Pearl and Stan got married at the Registry Office in Stokes Croft. My mother was very upset as Stanley should have got married in a Catholic church, but Pearl did not like the Catholic religion.

Pearl and Stan were very happy together and had a daughter Lorraine and a son Martin. They bought a house in Thornleigh Road, Horfield shortly after they were married and then around 1954, they moved to above a butcher's shop in Fishponds (opposite the Cross Hands pub) where Stan was the Manager. Later, they bought an 'Off licence' I think it was called 'The Queen's Head', but it didn't do very well once the supermarkets started selling alcohol, and Stan got very stressed and was put on anti-depressants.

Ron: Peter and I helped them move from Horfield to Fishponds as we were very friendly with them. It was on a Saturday morning, and we packed as much as we could before the removal van arrived. Stan still had not arrived home from work, so we had to help load all the furniture on our own. Pearl was furious. Just as we were about to drive off to the new place Stan arrived covered in oil. The chain on his motorbike had broken and he'd struggled to get it fixed. An AA man helped him and told him that he had bought a load of junk!

Mum: Stan and Pearl had to give up the 'Off licence' and they moved to Constable Road in Lockleaze which was not far from where Stan got another butcher's job in Gloucester Road. Pearl then used to mind children from 8.30 to 4 o'clock, Mondays to Fridays, while their mothers went to work, and she really enjoyed looking after the children. Lorraine and Martin are both married; both have had two children, but I do not see them very often. We have lived here at Hartcliffe for 16 Years and have many friends now that he has settled down at the two clubs we go to (the' 600' club and we also joined the Friday afternoon Club}.

When we first came to Hartcliffe we made friends and Mary Butt asked us to join the Friday afternoon club. Fred would not go and so I would not go either as we were happy in each other's company, visiting our parents and friends and having our family to visit us.

Then one day Mary Butt asked Fred again to join the club. She said 'Come and see how you'll enjoy it'. We went and he did enjoy it, but he had to sit with all women, one who he did not like.

So, he got talking to Joe and Wally. I told him to sit with Joe and they became grand friends. Joe's wife Ada and her sister Gladys also sat with them as well as Wally and his wife Ivy. He settled down to going every week. We had lovely outings and Joe, and Fred were happy together.

Ada's sister Gladys was the Leader of the Thursday Club which we also joined and had some wonderful times together. We went on many weeks' holidays with them but then Gladys was taken ill. She went into hospital at Manor Park but was very unhappy there. Then she came home and was taken to a hospital somewhere in the country.

We used to have a collection and when Ada and Joe went to see her they would take some beautiful flowers. Gladys passed away and was cremated at Southville Crematorium. We went by coach to her funeral; Fred was so upset. We went back to Ada and Joe's home after the funeral, had tea and then went home. Joe, Ada, Fred, Ivy, and Wally still sat together but Gladys was a big miss as Fred really thought a lot of her and they used to have a good laugh.

Joe was good fun and he loved gardening as they had a flat with a garden. Then Joe was taken ill, and Fred went up to see him several times. His wife Ada was a wonderful dressmaker and did alterations to clothes. I had been very ill and lost a lot of weight. Ada came down to measure my clothes to make them fit better.

Dorothy came over one Saturday morning and took Fred to see Joe, but Fred was so upset when he came home at how poorly Joe was. Joe died about two years ago in 1989 when he was nearly 90. Fred went to his funeral, but I could not go because I had just had a major operation and was too poorly to attend. Ada's brother was taken ill and died suddenly and was cremated at Bristol South crematorium. On the way back from the funeral Ada collapsed. I think that Joe's death and her brother's death both happening within six months was too much for her.

Ada's health just went, and she died suddenly shortly afterwards after going to her brother's funeral to be reunited with Joe. Fred was terribly upset as they were both very dear friends and Fred never seemed well again, but we had wonderful memories of them. All the flowers collected for Ada's funeral were taken to the hospital and to Hollybrook House. where so many disabled people live. They are cared for by wardens. At Christmas time both church and club members would go there, and they give a carol service and many Christmas parcels for the needy.

Fred would not go to the clubs on his own as I was so poorly, but we had many friends and so many visited us that we did enjoy their visits. Wally was another friend, and he was all right except that he was Polish, and we had difficulty understanding him speaking. He is nearly 90 and no longer attends the clubs as his health is very poor and a great anxiety to his wife Joy. He had a major operation like mine, and he can get very funny towards people and is not very good tempered. We occasionally meet him at the shops just up the road.

We enjoyed many day trips with the clubs, having a good sing song on the way home. We also used to go to a 'pensioners Day' at Ashton Court. We would be picked up by coach on a Sunday morning at about 11.30 and they would take our dinner with us. We had different lots of entertainment during the afternoon, and we were given orange drinks and ice cream at half price.

Maureen and her husband always brought the two boys with them, and we had a lovely afternoon together. We had other lovely afternoons and would then leave by coach about 5.00 p.m. and go to Weston for a fish and chip tea. We always looked forward to this Sunday and the weather was always hot.

In 1977 Jean and Ronald bought a village store (Swiss Valley Stores) in Clevedon with living accommodation and a very large garden. They did well at first and then supermarkets started to open, and trade slackened off. They closed the shop and made it back into a house. They have done it all up and it is beautiful and homely.

Mr and Mrs Smith remained great friends even after we left Southmead and one year Fred decided that he would like to go to Scotland. Mr and Mrs. Smith said that they would like to go as well, so we all went on Saturday morning about 9 o'clock. We travelled up to Gretna Green and saw many people waiting for a bride and groome. We saw the couple married over the anvil; it was very interesting. Many couples elope to marry there but they must live in the area for three weeks beforehand,

We travelled up to Scotland and had wonderful lodgings each place we stopped. We went to Edinburgh Castle which is very beautiful and interesting. After each crowd is let into a room the doors are locked behind them. The men were in their Scottish kilts and played music while the visitors were there. At each breakfast and evening meal the men are served first. A breakfast was two eggs, two rashers of bacon, sausages, tomatoes, and bread, butter and tea for the men and the women had just one egg bacon and sausage etc. so they certainly looked after the men!

We were very happy at all our lodgings as we went to the different places and stayed overnight. We did not book but found lodgings very easily. Only one night we thought we would have to sleep in the car but when we went into a cafe to get something to eat Fred asked the waitress if she knew of anywhere, we could get bed and breakfast. She said yes and Fred took her by car and booked in for the four of us.

Edith and Ern Smith were in one house and Fred and me were in another. We were made very welcome and when we went up to bed, we had two hot water bottles. The landlady said that all beds had hot water bottles and when we went down to breakfast there was a roaring fire. The landlady said that they always have a fire in the mornings, let it go out at mid-day and then relight it in the evenings.

We had wonderful weather and did about 2,000 miles from Bristol to Scotland and return in two weeks. We went to a beautiful park where the Scotsmen were dancing and playing the bagpipes. On our way home we stopped at Gloucester for the night. But In the morning we found that the landlady was very upset.

She had a couple there staying overnight and they had brought in their cases. After they left the next morning, she went to make their bed, but they had taken all the blankets, sheets, and pillowcases. As they had only stayed overnight, she did not have any address of where they lived. We spent the day in Gloucester and then travelled home.

We had a wonderful holiday and Mr and Mrs Smith, who always went on holiday with us, enjoyed themselves very much as well. They were always very good and helped to pay towards petrol.

Mrs Burt, who lived next door to Mr and Mrs Smith, was always at the door to see us off. Mrs Burt knew Fred when he was going to school in Trenchard Street. She was a very nice person, but her husband liked his drink, and they would quarrel a lot.

Mrs Burt had a large family (Kenneth was one of the boys) but one bad point she had was that she would leave home after her quarrels with her husband and stay away for weeks. During the war she would sit in her front room as she would not go down the air-raid shelter, but she was a kind person and very fond of all my children, as her family, our family and the Smith family all went to school together.

One morning Mrs Burt came to see me to ask me to lend her some money. I told her I was only on my war pension. She had her son with her and said that she wanted to buy him some boots as his toes were coming out of his broken ones. I felt sorry for her, and she offered me her wedding ring, but I told her I would never take my wedding ring off and I lent her £1. She promised to let me have it back the next day.

My rent man called, and I had to tell him that I couldn't pay my rent as I had lent a friend some money. It was the first time in all my married life that I had not the money to pay the rent. Mrs Smith came over to see me. She said Mrs Burt had left home. I told her that I had lent Mrs Burt £1 and she was very annoyed about this. She offered to lend me the money, but I told her that I would manage. It was a difficult time for me as I only got £4-10-0 9 (in old money) for me and four children. I managed to get the rent I owed together.

When the rent man called, I paid him the arrears. He asked me if I had got my money back from Mrs. Burt. I told him to mind his own business as he had his rent. Mrs Burt came back, and she was very annoyed with me for telling her husband that I had lent her money (I went to see him to see if he would pay me, but he couldn't or wouldn't). She paid me and I told her never to ask me again as I could not afford to lend people money out of my war pension.

She did not speak to me for some time but eventually we became friends again. After that I was always careful about lending anyone money and I have never been in debt although it was a struggle.

Ron: I remember Mr and Mrs. Smith very well and with great fondness. Mr Smith was also away during the war, and I remember one night Mum taking us across to her house and we all slept along the front room wall as far away from the window as possible.

Mr Smith was a slim, quite small man but he drove a huge 10 ton steamroller for Bristol Corporation. His main job was to flatten and smooth the tarmac and chippings when they resurfaced the roads. Whenever he was working close by we would always go to watch him manoeuvre the huge beast up and down the new surface.

He said that the smell of the tarmac meant he never got a cold and I have heard this from other people. Although he could drive a steam roller, he never took a driving test and he never ever drove a car. This was another reason, besides them being very good friends, that they went on holiday with Mum and Dad.

He had an allotment on the land across from the top of Coleford Road, in Doncaster Road. He was very good at gardening and grew a lot of vegetables as well as beautiful flowers. Sadly, he ended up suffering from Alzheimer's disease and when they found him one morning walking naked up Coleford Road, they had to put him in a home where he eventually died.

Both Mr and Mrs Smith were very good at decorating and did this to earn extra money. Mrs Smith ended up with very badly ulcerated legs and eventually had to give up her Council house and go to live in a warden-assisted flat in Henleaze Road because she could hardly walk.

Peter and I were very naughty one lunchtime whilst they were looking after us because we mixed the salt with the sugar, and it took them a little time before they twigged the problem. We got a good natured telling off from both mum and Mrs Smith, but I think they found it quite funny.

Mrs Smith had a sister who owned a grocery shop in Henleaze Road. Sometimes after we had been to the Saturday morning film club at the Orpheus cinema with Wally and Mervyn we had to walk home and pick up groceries for them.

We went to the children's cinema nearly every Saturday morning and mum would give a one shilling each (12d in old money and now equal to 5p). It was 1d each way on the bus, 9d for entrance money and the 1d left we would spend on a hot bread roll from Witt's bakery on Southmead Road. We would always scoop out the soft white bread in the middle and eat that first.

The cinema show would always start with a sing-along with indicators bouncing along under the words on the screen. This would be followed by cartoon films such as Tom and Jerry and then the morning would finish with a serial, mainly cowboys and Indians with such characters as Roy Rogers and Trigger, his horse, The Lone Ranger with his horse Silver and his Indian friend Tonto. The film would always end in suspense with the hero facing some horrendous death. At the start of the film the following week he had always made an amazing escape!

There was always cheering by the audience when the good guys were on the chase and boos for the bad guys. It was all great fun and we enjoyed it immensely.

The other highlight for us was Dick Barton 'special agent' with his friends Snowy and Jock. This was on the radio at 6.45 p.m., and we listened to it whenever we could. This programme was quickly followed by 'Journey into space' which enthralled and frightened us in equal measures. The theme tune is memorable.

In about 1949 a group of us lads were on Bristol Downs, one of our favourite haunts, when we saw a car with a large golden eagle on the top of it. A couple of men came across to us and said that a new comic 'The Eagle' was coming out and they gave us a load of coupons to get the magazine free and asked us to give them to our friends. Instead, we kept them ourselves and were able to get many weeks free. I must have been one of the first to join the Eagle club and you were given a badge in the shape of an eagle with a pin and hasp so you could wear it on your lapel. These are probably collectors' items by now but I do not know what happened to mine.

I also remember Mrs Burt very well. She was a very large lady and whenever I think of her, I think of the day that it was declared war was over when she was hanging out her bedroom window waving a 'Jerry pot' in the air which made us all laugh.

Back to Mum's story:

In the early Eighties my daughter-in-law Maureen went to see some relations in Canada for a couple of months.

They were chicken farmers. She was tremendously excited and impressed with Canada and the relatives sent money back home for Peter's fare so that he could join them for the rest of the holiday. While they were away, we went to Weston to look after the family which we loved doing.

Peter loved Canada as well. His job became insecure, and then he was made redundant and so the decision was virtually made for them. They sold everything and on 21st July 1984 they went to live there. By this time Maureen's dad had also died and Maureen also had problems with the rest of her family, and so she had no ties to keep her here.

They had difficulty getting a visa, but Peter wrote to their Prime Minister and that did the trick. It was heartbreaking for Fred and I them being so many miles away. They had a very bad first year and Peter later told me that they would have returned to England were it not for their two dogs that they had paid a lot of money to take out there with them. I hate those dogs.

Slowly their luck started to change. Maureen was able to do fostering and Peter got a job inspecting wood burning fires for an insurance company. He had to go back to college for training and get a 'certificate of competence' before he was able to do it.

They have bought a house at Sorrento, and it seems a lovely place. Steven has his own house and business; Andrew has just bought his house and is getting married next September 1902. Karen has graduated and is doing well, and Sally Ann is also getting on OK.

Two years ago, Maureen, Peter, and Sally Ann and a boy they are fostering came to England for three weeks' holiday. They stayed with Maureen's sister (Shirley) at Withywood as they have a large house. Peter and Maureen came to see Fred and me and we had a lovely time. We had a lovely party with family and friends at Ronald's house in Clevedon.

Mrs Davies (Blod), a friend of mine wanted to see Peter and Maureen, so one Friday morning I went with Peter and Maureen to visit her. Sally Ann my granddaughter and the boy that Peter had adopted stayed with Fred as there was not enough room in the car for all of us. Blod and I worked together at Mrs Buckland's school.

Blod made us very welcome, but we could only spare her an hour as Peter and Maureen had so many friends to see and time goes by so quickly when you are visiting. On our way home Maureen went into the fish and chip shop in Parson Street and we took our dinners home. Fred had the table laid and we had a wonderful time together.

Up to now, Maureen and Peter have taken care of about 16 foster children who have then gone elsewhere. She now has four children who are brothers and sisters who they are going to keep and possibly adopt for good. Everyone is pleased about this.

They have done a wonderful job as many of the children were so badly treated and it is heart-warming the way they have recovered. We had a lovely time while they were over here, and all the family met up and we had a party. They visited many other friends but called in every day to see us. I miss them all so very much and was heart-broken when they went back, but I am so pleased that they have all done well.

I wish that I could fly to see them, but I don't like aeroplanes and it would cost a lot to go although I know my family would help me.

I am now writing and bringing you up to date on my brothers and sisters.

My brother Bill is 76. He is getting very absent minded and goes to a day centre. His wife Doreen is very nice but is also not in good health. Bill was a very good dancer and played the accordion. He was a driver on the buses for many years but had to give up when he developed cataracts in his eyes. He had them removed and then went to work at the infirmary as a porter.

He finally got so bad that first they put him in a retirement home at the top of Longcross, Lawrence Weston, near Blaise Castle and then, when he became too difficult to handle, into Ham Green Hospital.

Ron: I went to visit Bill both in Lawrence Weston and in Ham Green Hospital, but he could not remember anyone. The last time I saw him he told me that earlier that day he had driven all the people in the hospital on a coach trip to the seaside and they had a lovely time. It was pitiful to see him like that, he was desperately thin, but he seemed happy.

Mum: My brother Arthur is 68 and was forced to retire about seven years ago when he had a stroke. He is getting on well and his wife Iris is so lovely. She was very ill in her younger days and was not allowed to have children so neither of my elder brothers had any.

Ron: It was not until the 60 years' anniversary of the Normandy landings that our family discovered at a party, we were holding in our garden, that Arthur had been involved as part of the operation to land on 'Gold' Beach. He fought his way through to Berlin and was the driver of a gun carrier. Whilst in Berlin he had to guard Hess in Spandau Prison.

Mum: My youngest brother, Stanley, died about seven years ago, he was very ill in Frenchay Hospital. He had a wife, Pearl and they had two children: a daughter Lorraine and a son Martin. One is working, and Martin is still at school.

Ron: I got on very well with Stan and he was much more like an older brother than an uncle. I first remember him when they lived in Holton Road. He was forced to go to the Catholic Church which he hated. He was always riding his bike and with his small round glasses looked quite studious. He carved me a small boat out of wood which I thought was marvellous.

As Peter and I got older we treated him as a best friend and often went out with him. My sister Flo thought that he was a bad influence on us, but we thought he was wonderful fun. After he married Pearl and lived above the butcher's shop in Fishponds, we would go every Christmas and help to pluck the large number of Christmas chickens and turkeys for his customers. He always rewarded us by cooking the best steak in the shop with chips.

Just after we were married, Jean and I went with Stan and Pearl to London to see the Tower and had a good day with them. Whenever Lorraine comes to our annual family get together and there is someone new she has not met before, she will invariably tell them that when she was a baby in her pram, I saved her life. That's a different story.

Mum: My sister Flo married George Catley and they have a son, Georgie and a daughter, Pat who both now have their own children. Flo is 79 and George is about 83. Their health is not too good, but they are very happy together and I visit them when I possibly can. George was always full of fun, and they always came to our parties. The whole family would turn up on their motorbike and sidecar together with their paraphernalia and film projector equipment.

George had a lot of films and would entertain the children (and the adults!) with films such as Popeye and Olive Oyl. He worked as a Fireman at the Bristol Aircraft Corporation and saw many horrendous things during the war.

My sister Violet (Vi) is lovely. She married Vernon St. Claire, and they have a son, Stephen, and a daughter, Margaret. She also lost a baby at birth which was very traumatic for me as well because I was helping to look after her at the time, in the same way that she had cared for me during the war.

She used to work in Stokes Croft making toys and she worked very hard. Whilst she was living with Mum and Dad at Holton Road, she fell in love with a man close to where she lived. Both Mum and Dad were very upset about this and because she would not give him up and she left home. (See note below).

I was deeply upset about it as my parents were wonderful to us all. I kept in touch with her and asked her to go back home, but she would not give him up. She used to come to visit me at Southmead and then one day she came to tell me she had finished with him. I told her to go back to Mum and Dad, but she refused to return home.

She gave up her job toy making toys and became a conductress on the trams. She started courting Vernon (Vern) again and I told her again to go back to Mum's. I had a talk with my mother, and she was so pleased to know that Vi wanted to return home. So, I met Vi and took her back to Mum and Dad's house and everything was fine again. I know how heartbroken my parents were, but I never had any quarrel with Vi and we were all friendly with her. I knew one day she would come home to our parents. Vi and Vernon were married, and they have been very happy together. We have had some lovely times with them.

Ron: I grew up living with a very different version of the above events which Mum is 'whitewashing' to protect her parents. Vern is black and this caused a huge rift between Vi and her parents. In these days, being black would not have reflected as badly on Mum's parents by her neighbours as it did back in the 1940s. I can understand their dilemma to some degree because in 1969 we were selling our house in Coronation Road. The estate agent brought round a black man and his wife to view our property.

Immediately they left, our next-door neighbour was hammering on our front door. She watched everything we did from behind her curtains and once complained that my brother-in-law was obstructing her view by parking his van outside her property! She told me in a very forthright manner that I was not to sell the house to a n***** as it would lower the value of her property.

I kept my temper and politely told her that it was out of my hands because it was the estate agent's job to arrange the sale and there were new race equality laws that I had to abide by. She left in a huff and that was the last time we spoke because we moved to Easton in Gordano not long afterwards. The couple agreed to buy our house and I was happy to sell it to them.

The mortgage company refused their application because even though he worked for British Rail and earned a good wage, a lot of it came from overtime which they would not include in their financial assessment. His wife's earnings were also not considered in those days. We were fortunate to get a sale agreed very quickly to a young couple who were getting married and their parents who lived less than a quarter of a mile away was buying it for them.

The reconciliation did not come until after the war and Vern had returned from POW camp in a terrible state. They got married and it was after that mum 'brokered' a deal. Both my sisters have a very different opinion of Granny Croome and are writing their own memoirs and I have no doubt it will be reflected there!

Mum: When Fred was 80 years old, all the family gave him a wonderful party which we had at Deborah's house (Dot's daughter). We didn't know anything about it until we arrived there. All the families were there, and we had a lovely time. Fred had a lovely birthday cake that Jean had specially made in the shape of a pair of woman's breasts, which he thought was very funny.

The family put together and bought him a beautiful wireless and many other presents. Fred loved his music and really enjoyed his presents; we have so many happy memories to look back on.

When I was 80 my son Ron and my daughters gave me a party at his house. It was held on a Sunday afternoon as I had gone through a major operation in the June, and I was very weak.

I did not stay late but we still had a wonderful time. Flo and Den took Fred and me to the party, but as we went down the M5 motorway there was a bad traffic jam and instead of getting there at 3 o'clock as arranged, we did not get there until nearly four. Flo had to ring Ron to let him know what had happened as all the visitors had got there early to surprise me.

As I have said many times, we have such wonderful memories. Nearly every Bank holiday Sunday the whole family would go out in our cars for the day. We would leave home about 10 a.m. and take a picnic with us. We would play rounders and other games and the grandchildren would have a wonderful time. I now have ten grandchildren and three great grandchildren altogether and am very proud of all our families and have a wonderful time when we meet.

My eldest grandchild is Flo's daughter, Carol who was born in 1956. Carol was always very shy but then she started work with the Port of Bristol Authority and went out for a while with a boy called Phillip Coward who was a relative of the famous Noel Coward.

Ron: Philip Coward lived on his parents' farm and one day we were all out at a restaurant together and we were sat opposite Carol and Philip. He looked at Jean and said she had lovely brown eyes, just like my cow daisy. He could not understand why we were in fits of laughter!

Mum: The relationship did not last very long and then she joined the Royal Air Force and whilst in there met her husband Gordon who was also serving in the forces. They got married in a church at Lawrence Weston, Bristol and it was a beautiful wedding. We had the usual wedding photos taken by a professional photographer, but they were told the following week that none of the photos had come out.

Shortly afterwards on a Sunday, the photographer arranged for those who could, to go back to the church and the photographs were taken again. They even laid on a buffet for everyone and this time the photos came out al lright. Unfortunately, not everyone was able to attend and so some are missing from the photographs.

Ron: See my poem, Carol's second wedding.

Mum: On the evening of the wedding, we all went to a celebration party in a hall on the Downs and had a wonderful time finishing about 11.00 pm. Carol and Gordon are still in the Royal Air Force and living very happily in their own house in Gloucester.

My second eldest grandchild is Flo's son Philip who is two years younger than Carol. The first girl he married was the daughter of Roger Marcus, a well known and very rich scrap dealer from Bristol, (his vehicles were number plated RM1, RM2 etc.) Their reception was a very large affair in the posh hotel on the Bristol harbour waterfront (now, in 2007, called Jury's). Unfortunately, the marriage did not last very long.

His second marriage was to Jayne, and again it was a lovely wedding and she looked beautiful in her wedding dress. It took place in the church on the main Staple Hill Road. We went in the evening to yet another lovely reception at the Tracey Park golf club where many friends who could not get to the wedding came. We had dancing and a sing song, and really enjoyed it, getting home about midnight. Fred was so happy at these receptions and talked to many friends we had not seen for some time.

My third grandchild is Beverly, the daughter of Jean and Ron who was born on the 14 June 1962. Beverly is married to Trevor Baker and their wedding took place at All Saints Church in Clevedon. The weather was awful, and it rained the whole day, but it was a very happy occasion, and we did not let the weather spoil it. We had the reception in the Community Hall and went back there again in the evening for a party for the rest of their friends. We stayed at Jean and Ron's in between.

They are a lovely couple and have just bought a house in Clevedon, near to the sea front. They have such beautiful views overlooking the sea. They both have good jobs and enjoy their work although they work long hours. Beverly has an excellent job at the British Gas Company in Keynsham, and she is one of the heads of section there.

My next eldest grandchild (fourth) is Dorothy and Bryan's daughter, Deborah, who was born in 1963. She is married to Oliver Clarke (Ollie) and they also had a lovely wedding, wedding reception, and an evening party for their other friends. Ollie's grandparents came to the wedding and are very nice and homely. They are a lovely couple and have their own house in Almondsbury.

Stephen, Maureen, and Peter's son was also born in 1963 and is a shy and quiet boy. He spends many hours on the computer and has invented some computer games. He has now taken this up as a career in Canada and has become very rich.

Martin, the son of Jean and Ron, was born next and married Aurora (Bhot or Bhebot) who is from the Philippines. She comes from a very large Protestant family, and they met and fell in love whilst Martin was serving with the army in Cyprus. They were married in Manila and Jean and Ron travelled there to see the wedding. Felipinos class themselves as 'brown people' as shown on their birth certificates and passports and they are very attractive people.

Apparently, it was a wonderful wedding but different from ours as the parents take no part in the ceremony. Aurora's parents were very nice and made Jean and Ron very welcome. They were provided with guards wherever they went because of the difficult political situation in the country at that time.

Ron: This was during the time when President Marcos had been overthrown and Corrie Okino had become President after Marcos had her husband assassinated and there were some very scary moments – I have given a full description of this in my poem 'Martin's wedding in the Philippines.'

Mum: On 29 August 1989 Francia, Martin and Aurora's (Bhot's) daughter, was two years old and so, on the first of September, they had a lovely birthday party for her. A lot of Bhot's friends came to the party. There were about 40 altogether, and several beautiful young babies. They are all so friendly and I had a wonderful time.

The family and friends arrived about 3 o'clock. Ron and Jean have a beautiful garden and all the trees were decorated with flags and balloons. They had a barbeque and a lot of them were doing the cooking. They eat different foods that I cannot take, so Jean did me a nice salad with ham and pork pie.

They had a sing song and dancing in the evening and all the trees were lit up with lights and a great canopy to cover the garden so if it rained, we would be under cover. But it was a beautiful day, very hot and in the evening cool enough to sit out until 10.30 p.m.

Quite a few went home, as they had young children and about a dozen slept at Ron and Jean's, bringing their sleeping bags. Some of the men had to go back to their ship at Avonmouth. We all enjoyed it, and I was made so welcome. I hope one day I will be able to meet some of them again and really enjoy their company. They are a friendly crowd and plenty of happiness was had.

Ron: There was a cable laying ship that regularly docked at Avonmouth Docks and quite a few of the crew were from the Philippines. They were great friends of Bhot's and would frequently visit our house. They adored Jean and my mum and would serenade them. We missed all this and the friendship of the Philippine community when Bhot and Martin separated and finally divorced.

Mum: Richard, Dot, and Bryan's son was born next. He is not yet married but lives with Denise in their own house. He works very hard as a builder and is a good footballer; I often go to watch him play when the weather permits.

Karen, Andrew, and Sally Ann were the last of the grandchildren to be born and are Maureen and Peter's children. As I have already said they went to Canada when they were quite young, and I greatly regret having missed a lot of their growing up.

I have two great grandchildren, Alexander and James, sons of Philip and Jayne. They are lovely children. Flo, and Den (Philip's mother and father) have them for weekends as Phil and Jayne are now divorced. It is so sad because family life is so rewarding and to see your children grow up brings great happiness.

Jayne sometimes comes to see me at Flo's. I feel very sorry for Jayne and Phil because they don't know what they are missing in the companionship they could have enjoyed with each other and the joy of bringing up two sons. Alexander is three and goes to play school and James is 18 months. James took quite a time to walk, so Jayne took him to a special doctor. He has physiotherapy and must wear special boots. He can now walk about 12 steps on his own. He is very shy but when he gets used to you, he is very friendly. Alexander likes playing football and Flo and Den take them to Blaise Castle and different seaside places. He loves to play football with the family and to slide down the slider with James.

I go to Flo and Den's every three weeks for the weekend and when we go to Blaise Castle Flo, and I sit and watch them all play. The boys generally sleep in the afternoon and then Phil takes them home to Jayne at about 6 o'clock after we have had our Sunday meal. Sometimes Carol and Gordon come down on a Sunday afternoon as well and we all go out together. Alexander goes to play school three mornings a week. He was very upset when he first went, but now he loves it as he has something to learn and other children to be friendly with.

Flo and Den are wonderful grandparents, and it nearly broke their hearts when they heard the news of Phil and

Jayne parting. Carol and Gordon live in Gloucester and sometimes on a Saturday Flo and Den and the grandchildren go to visit them. Gordon is in the Royal air Force in Gloucester and Carol works in an office although at one time she was also in the Air Force. I love all my family and it gives me great happiness to be with them all.

Flo works at the Dental Clinic in Shirehampton from 8.30 to 5.00 p.m. Her boss, Peter, is very nice. Some days Flo and her boss visit old folks homes to care for the aged who cannot get to the clinic. Flo enjoys working with old folk and some are very friendly, but others do not want their teeth seen to.

Peter is very understanding, and the folk normally look forward to his next visit. He came to see Fred once as he was having trouble with his teeth. Fred did not like going to the dentist because when he had some of his teeth out, he was not at all happy with the dentist. I now take it in turns to go to Dorothy and Bryan's, Flo and Den's, and Ron and Jean's for the weekends.

For some time during 1988 I had been feeling poorly and so my doctor made an appointment for me to see a doctor at the BRI. I had different X-rays and they found I had a hiatus hernia. So, I had to visit the BRI very often having different X-rays and Barium Meal.

I went into hospital in January 1989, then again in March and again on 6 June. The doctor said I would not come home until they found out what was wrong with me. I had all kinds of X-rays taken and on 17 June I had a very major operation. I was very ill, and the family were only allowed short visits.

I went into the operating theatre at 8.30 in the morning and was not put back into the ward until 6.30 in the evening. Dorothy came in about 5 o'clock and could not find my bed: they had taken me to the theatre on it. She went upstairs to find a phone but both phones were out of use. I was told after I was better that Dorothy thought that I had died.

She was crying and as they brought me out of theatre, I saw her, and the nurse and I told her I was all right. It was a terrible time for Fred as he visited me every day. Ron brought him at dinner times, and he used to go to the cafe and have a cup of tea and something to eat. Dorothy and Flo came on alternate days and took Fred home each evening.

It was a great worry to the family as Fred was so poorly and not eating food. He would alternate his weekends between the girls and Ron, and they would bring him in to see me.

Ron: Dad was very frail and walking with a stick. Several times he almost fell over and it was difficult getting him into and out of the car. The walking stick he used belonged to his grandfather and it is one of my prized possessions.

Mum: I can't remember the first week after my operation, just seeing faces as I had drips through my nose and stomach. Fred used to make fun of me. He used to call me 'Elephant Nose' as the drip from my nose looked like an elephant's trunk. As the days went by, I felt stronger and then one of the nurses said that they were going to teach me how to walk again.

Two nurses helped me out of bed and very slowly I walked. The other patients were so encouraging to see me try to walk by catching hold of the two nurses, but after a short while they said that was enough and brought me back to bed in a wheelchair. The nurses walked me for nearly a week, and then told me I had to walk by myself. I was really scared but the other patients cheered me on and finally I was able to walk from the bottom to the top of the ward without a wheelchair.

It was lovely to feel my legs again and realise that each day I was nearer to coming home. I went into hospital on 6 June and came home on 17 July 1989. When I arrived home by ambulance, I was taken upstairs to our flat in the lift by two ambulance men. It was a wonderful moment for me to be home again with Fred and he had the table full of beautiful flowers to welcome me.

And it was extra special because 20 July was our 58th wedding anniversary. We were married on July 20, 1931.

My family looked after Fred and me and many friends visited us. After two weeks of being at home I told Fred that I would like to go out for some fresh air. I was so nervous when I got into the lift. Fred walked me a short way across the road and back. I was exhausted and felt I didn't want to go walking again. Day by day, weather permitting, I used to go for short walks, across to the garage opposite the flats. The family were wonderful and would take us out.

I was an outpatient at the BRI. An ambulance would come to take me down in the wheelchair, as we lived on the fifth floor of the block of flats. We would have a good laugh; the ambulance men were wonderful. Fred would get the dinner ready. I would go about 9 o'clock in the morning and arrive home about one o'clock. They would take the people living the furthest away home first; we would have a bit of fun and I enjoyed seeing so many people and enjoying their company.

Fred was a wonderful husband and father. We all did not realise that he was so poorly. When I came home from hospital, I could not do anything to help him. He kept our home beautiful. A lady from the 'home help' came to see me as the ward sister at the BRI said I needed help. She was very abrupt and wanted me to let them do my washing as they preferred washing to cleaning.

I told them 'no'! they could not do my washing as my two daughters had already been doing my it for over a year, as I was an outpatient at the BRI for over a year before my operation. The lady was very annoyed and told me that if that was the case, she didn't think I would get any help. That was on a Thursday morning and when Flo and Den came over on the Saturday, I told them. So, they vacuumed through the flat and dusted and then took home the washing.

Dorothy and Flo did our heavy shopping, but Fred used to go to the shops for smaller odds and ends, but he had to walk with a stick and was very unsure of walking without one. On the Monday morning following that weekend a 'home help' called and Fred asked her to come in. I said that there was nothing for her to do as my family had done it on the weekend because we did not think we would be getting any help.

She said that she could not go back without doing something so Fred asked her to get up and clean the curtain rail as he could not pull the curtains together properly. She got up and did it and told us not to report her because she was not supposed to stand on steps. Fred said that he would not report her as it was not her fault that there was nothing for her to do. For some time, we had regular 'home help' on a Wednesday just vacuuming, no dusting.

Ron: The stress on the family was considerable, but it was fortunate that we could all drive and all play our part. I was able to get extra phone assistance to make it easier for them to contact us in an emergency. Dot and Flo were both brilliant because by this time mum had a colostomy bag fitted, which she detested, and would only talk to the girls about it.

Mum: Fred struggled on day by day not telling me or the family how poorly he was. We had to have meals on wheels from Monday to Friday, it cost me £1.50 each day. Fred didn't like the meals as when he was in the Royal air Force, he had to eat so many carrots. My appetite was very poor, and we wasted a lot of our dinners. I would give Fred some of my dinner and have his carrots.

He was so sick after his dinners that I asked the 'home help' to cancel them and told her that he couldn't eat so many carrots and so much gravy. She cancelled three dinners out of five as she didn't want to take our names off the list as winter was coming, and we may not be able to get our names back it. We gave it another week and then cancelled the dinners.

I would do the vegetables sitting down and Fred would wash them and put them on to cook. He would fry whatever meat we had. I would bake cakes sitting down and we managed quite well, and the girls, Ron and Jean would help us when needed.

Still Fred had these bilious attacks. He had earache very bad and when he went to see Dr. Greenwood, she gave him tablets and something to put in his ears. Fred was very stubborn as he would not tell Dr. Greenwood how poorly he was. I had to send for Dr. Greenwood several times and told her how he was, but he wouldn't admit how painful his ear was.

He would hold his head and very often walk from one room to another. Some days it would go, and he would be OK. Fred still went shopping. I could not walk far so when I saw him coming down the road, I would do my short walk to the garage opposite our flats. We had a shopping trolley which Fred could use as he always had to walk with a stick.

Fred enjoyed going up the shops as he met so many friends and enjoyed a good chat with them. When I went into hospital, he said he had several dinners at the Friday club: he didn't really enjoy them, but the company was good for him

Many friends came to see us, but he liked quietness, and he would doze off to sleep in the afternoons. I really thought that because he had done so much visiting coming into hospital to see me, that was why he was so tired, not realising how poorly he was as he never complained. If you asked him how he was, he was always 'allright'.

Fred normally loved company but as each day passed, he would rather be on our own. The family were marvellous and came to see us, but still not realising he was feeling so ill. He used to sleep a lot in the afternoons, and I would watch television. I tried to make conversation with him, but he just said yes or no.

Ron: Up to about here, Mum's writing was very clear, concise, and consistent in size. From now on it gets larger and larger and I can only guess why.

Mum: I remember one Wednesday Fred's sister Gladys came to see us. She visited us once a month and would often ring us in between times. I cooked dinner and called Fred to let me know how much dinner he wanted as he was eating so little. He came out into the kitchen and told me that what I had put on his plate was enough. Gladys picked it up and carried it in for him. Gladys had been a nurse and she came back out into the kitchen and said that it was not enough to keep a fly alive. I told her that he would not even eat all of that.

After dinner he kept dozing off even though I tried to keep him awake while Gladys was there. Gladys told me on her way out that she was fearful for Fred's future and advised me to contact the doctor urgently.

The last week before he was taken into hospital, he went to bed about 9 o'clock. I washed up our supper cups and went into the bathroom to get ready for bed as owing to my illness I had to see to myself (clean a colostomy bag). Fred would say 'you can have a read', but I said no as I knew he was so tired.

He was in so much pain with his ear that he would get back out of bed and go into the front room and sit there. We had a blanket which I kept on the settee so that when he was in the front room, he could wrap it around himself. After a while he would come back to bed.

Fred would have his breakfast in bed and then go back to sleep. I kept going into the bedroom as I was so worried about him. I would make him a cup of tea about mid morning, and then he would go off to sleep again. Sometimes he would have his dinner in bed, get up after dinner and sit in his dressing gown with the blanket around himself.

I often phoned Dr. Greenwood but there was little she could do. Each time she came, Fred would say he was better and refused to tell her about the bad nights he had.

I am certain that his greatest fear was going into hospital and never coming out again.

Dr. Greenwood told me to send for her anytime day or night as she fully understood the situation. Dorothy and Flo were ever so good as they came and did my shopping as Fred was so poorly, he could no longer get to the shops. Ron came without fail every Wednesday lunchtime. He told them all that he was much better, but none of them believed him anymore.

Ron: It was a desperate time for all of us. Dad really should have been in hospital, but we all knew that would be the end for him. We all had families to look after, jobs to go to at a time when the UK was in a desperate situation. We were all completely worn out.

Mum: On 11th April 1990 Dr. Greenwood rang me to say that she was going away for Easter. She told me that if I needed a doctor for Fred to ask for a certain doctor who she had told how poorly Fred was. April 13th was Good Friday and Peter's birthday in Canada. Fred slept most of the day. He had breakfast in bed and then again went back to sleep.

It was such a worrying day, but he would not let me call the doctor. About 9 o'clock in the evening I asked him if he was going to bed. He was very irritable and shouted that he would go when he was ready. As he had been in bed each night by 9 o'clock I thought that he would be ready to go.

I told him I was going to the bathroom as since my operation I had to see to myself. About 10 o'clock I went into

273

the front room to speak to him and told him I was going to bed. I was so worried, so I had a read. I then looked through the living room door and he was laying the tablecloth for tomorrow's breakfast. As he had had breakfast in bed every day, I thought he imagined that he was getting up in the morning. He finished laying the table and he caught hold of the chairs and slowly walked to the door. I went into the bedroom as I did not want him to know I was watching him.

He went into the bathroom and when I heard him coming out, I went and helped him walk into the bedroom. It was pitiful to see him in so much pain. We both settled down, he told me to have a read, but I said I was tired. About 3 o'clock in the morning I heard Fred call me; I thought he was in the sitting room in his usual place. It was in darkness, and I said 'where are you'? I found him in the bathroom leaning over the bath. He was soaking wet, so I took off his pyjamas and wiped him dry.

I got him fresh pyjamas, but I could not raise him up from the bath. I told him he must try, as having this major operation I could not do any lifting. I phoned Dorothy about 4 o'clock in the morning and she came straight over. Bryan wanted to come with her, but she told him to stay home as he had to go into work in the morning.

I managed to get Fred sat on a stool, and then I got a chair and he managed to sit on it. I told him I could not help him as owing to my operation I was not able to lift him. Dorothy arrived and we managed to get him into bed. I phoned the emergency doctor, and he was not long in coming. Dorothy helped the doctor to get him to stand up, and the doctor said that Fred had suffered a mild stroke.

Dorothy told the doctor about my operation, and he said that Fred must go into hospital. Fred looked so ill and could not really understand what was going on. I told him he had to go to hospital for a few days. The ambulance arrived and I was shocked when they said that he had to go Manor Park Hospital as the BRI had no beds.

We arrived at Manor Park Hospital at about 6 o'clock in the morning. I went in the ambulance with Fred and Dorothy followed in her car. The doctors at Manor Park were very nice and the Sister told me not to worry. After his examination we were allowed to see him. The Sister said to ring about 10 o'clock and she would let us know which ward he was in.

He looked so bewildered I don't think he realised where he was. We stayed a little while, then we went back to Dorothy's at about 8.00 a.m. Bryan was just going to work. Dorothy rang Flo and Ron to tell them about Fred.

Dorothy rang Manor Park Hospital and was told what ward Fred was in, and we were told that we could go in right away to see him. He was pleased to see us but could not understand what had happened. We stayed about an hour with him and then went back home to ring the family to let them know what ward Fred had been admitted into.

Dorothy and I went back to Manor Park. Fred looked so ill and confused. He was looking at the door, as the nurse had told him we were coming in to see him. He was in a very nice ward and the nurses were very kind to him. The Sister was also very nice and took us to see him. We told him that it was for his own good that he was in hospital although I don't think he realised what was going on

Flo, Ron, and the family all came to see him during that first time he arrived at Manor Park. We then arranged for someone to go in during the afternoon and some in the evenings. Owing to my illness I could not go in alone and so the family took it in turns to take me in each day.

He settled down in Manor Park and the nurses were very kind. His ear was very painful, and they were not able to determine the cause. Sometimes he would sit in a chair besides his bed. They took him to the dining room for his meals although he was very poor at eating.

He was in Manor Park about ten days and then he was moved to the General Hospital. It was much easier for me as I could go in every afternoon by bus to see him. The family arranged the evening visits and many of our family, Fred's sister Gladys, and my sisters and brothers all visited him because he was greatly loved.

Ron: I had an amazing call from the hospital administration while I was at work telling me that they needed dad's bed, but there were no ambulances available to take him to the General Hospital. Would I be able to take him there in my car? How could they possibly ask me to do this? Dad was a very sick man prone to strokes. Getting him into my car would be difficult enough, but what could I do if he took a turn for the worse

I refused, but this was the state the NHS was in at that time. People found it difficult to believe that I had even been asked to do such a thing.

Arthur and Iris would go in the afternoon as well as Vi and Vern, leaving the evenings free for our family. He was very happy at the General Hospital and the nurses were wonderful to him. I would go to see him about 2.30pm and go home by bus about 5 o'clock which gave him time to rest before the evening visitors. Fred was greatly respected by all who met him although in so much pain.

He loved to talk to everyone and the nurses and Dr. Pocock were wonderful to him.

Dr. Pocock asked me and my children to go to see him one Wednesday morning. Dorothy, Flo, Ron, and I sat in the corridor. Fred could not see us, but we could see him. Dr. Pocock explained about Fred's illness. He said he was like a trunk of a tree with the branches at the side and they did not know which was good or bad branches.

Fred had so many X-rays and then he had a scan. He told me he was scared as he went round and round. He couldn't eat and so he was put on a drip. He was getting so thin. Ron and Jean had booked to fly to Portugal for two weeks, but Ron was so worried that he wanted to cancel their holiday.

I told him to go as Dad could still be alive when they got back. I promised him that if Dad was worse, we would get in touch with Martin. Fred was such a wonderful patient, and the nurses loved him dearly. Ron and Jean went to Portugal, but it was an anxious time for them being so many miles from home.

Then Fred wanted to come home and Dorothy and I went to see him. He tried to get out of bed but having his drips on both arms he couldn't manage it. He said to Dorothy 'you have your car, you can do it.' Dorothy said she would ask the Sister. The Sister came to Fred and told him he must stay until the drips were taken out.

We knew Fred was so ill, and the Sister said he would not be able to come home as, owing to my operation I could not help him. We were told that he would not be able to stay at the General Hospital and as good as Manor Park Hospital was to him we did not want him to go back there.

Flo was terribly upset when Dorothy rang her and told her dad was being taken back to Manor Park, but as I explained to her there was no room at the BRI or the General Hospital. Flo settled down and was much happier when we phoned her and told her that they were going to let Dad stay at the General.

Each day we visited him he looked so ill. He tried to smile, but he had another slight stroke which made his mouth slant even more. He could not talk to us, so we took to writing paper and pen. We would talk to him, and he would try to write and answer back. The Sister was very good and would come over to help us.

It was heartbreaking to see him try because he could not do it. He was happy in his own way because he understood us although we did not understand him. Ron and Jean went to Portugal but did not enjoy their holiday knowing Dad was so ill.

Ron: Whether to go on holiday was one of the most difficult decisions we have ever had to make. We knew that Dad was very ill but had no idea whether he was going to die or would recover. We were also having quite a tough time what with mum and Dad needing a lot of support and work being extremely difficult.

Margaret Thatcher's privatisation of services were in full swing and none of us knew whether our jobs were safe, and I was in the process of making 120 grounds workers redundant following the loss the of the Education school's grounds maintenance to the firm Brophy These were two Irish brothers who put in unsustainable ridiculously bids and who were given the work because all departments had to cut budgets. Many of the Council workers were 'green card' persons: men or women who were employed on a government subsidy and would not get work outside of a protected environment.

Making these very good people redundant with virtually no hope of ever working again I found offensive and distressing and, as Personnel Manager, it was my task to see it through. I had grown men crying in my office because they thought they were secure for life and now faced redundancy, desperate times and, in some cases, financial ruin.

I turned grey in less than a year and only realised it when I went into Avon House for a meeting. I said hello to a friend and colleague in the corridor, who I had not seen in a good while because I was working in Brislington depot, and he was in Avon House North. He walked passed me as I spoke and then he turned around and said: 'Good God Ron, I didn't recognise you as you are so grey!'

We were also having problems with the house which we were trying to renovate. The staircase was about to collapse because it had been affected by dry rot and again, we were we were facing a huge bill. (Note: Bev's husband Trevor was a star; just look at the photos of us removing the black plaster – we looked like chimney sweeps!). Mum was very aware of these problems and the stress we were under as we talked frequently about everything, and therefore she insisted that we went.

We were staying in Monte Gordo and in those days, communication was very difficult and expensive, so we were unable to get information. Dad was continually on our minds, and we were also really worried about Mum who was still recovering from her very major operation for bowel cancer.

The lowest point for me came when we were in a cafe very close to the Spanish border which was in walking distance from out hotel. I was listening to Neil Diamond singing 'Hello my friend, hello', and I was reduced to tears. I had to look away out of the window so that Jean would not see me crying. I broke down again in a park a couple of days later and this time Jean saw me and could not really understand why I was so upset. Even today I choke up whenever I hear Neil Diamond singing that song.

Mum: On May 30th, 1990, at about 5 o'clock in the morning I had a phone call from Dorothy telling me to get ready as the Sister at the General Hospital had phoned and asked for the family to go in. Dorothy rang Flo and Flo rang Martin as he was going to pick Jean and Ron up from the airport later that day, as they were coming home from Portugal.

Dorothy came over for me and we met up with Flo and Dennis outside the General Hospital. When we got to the ward Fred was sat up in bed smiling. He was so pleased to see us but couldn't understand why we had come in. Flo, Den, Dorothy, and I sat with him. Some went out to let Bryan, Deborah and Richard come in.

We stayed with him until 8.30 a.m. and then went home to have breakfast. We went back again about 10 o'clock and left at 12 o'clock to have dinner, then back again until 4.30 p.m. when I felt so poorly that I had to go outside. The Sister got me some water and sat with me.

Fred asked Dorothy where I was; he thought I had gone to the 'ladies. I came back and tried hard to smile. Fred asked me if I was all right, and I said 'yes' and he said that I should go home.

I promised to go back, but the Sister said that if there was any change in him she would phone Dorothy. I felt so ill that Dorothy took me to her home.

During that time Martin was at Bristol airport waiting for Ron and Jean to arrive back from holiday. When Ron and Jean arrived, they were escorted straight through Customs as Martin had got in touch with someone at the airport.

Ron: As we arrived in the luggage reclamation area there was a message over the Tannoy system asking us to make ourselves known to an official. They were excellent and they helped us to retrieve our bags and we were through passport control within minutes and Martin was waiting in reception. He explained how serious the situation was and drove us straight to hospital.

We were shocked at the sight of Dad when we arrived. His mouth was crooked from the latest stroke, and they had stitched one of his eyes shut as he could not close it himself. He was on a drip, and he was so frail, but as usual tried to be humorous and to say he was all right. I had my camera ready, and we joked that he should have his picture taken so that when he came home, he could see what he looked like!

We still have that photograph of Jean sat with him on the bed and I still wonder whether I should destroy it, as he looks terrible. However, it is part of history and if I destroy it, it is lost forever.

Mum: Ron and Jean came straight from the hospital to see me, had something to eat and then went home to Clevedon. Ron said he would pop into hospital again that day, but I told him to go home and rest after all that travelling. At about 5.30 p.m. Dorothy rang the hospital again to see how Fred was. The Sister asked who Ronald was as Fred was asking for him. Dorothy explained that it was his son, and she immediately rang Ron who had just got home. Ron went straight back down to the General Hospital to see what Fred wanted.

Fred was very confused and said that the hospital had got his address wrong, and they were showing it as Flat 18 instead of Flat 34. Ron went across to see the Sister who then brought her book over to show Fred that she had the right address in it. The reason he was worried about the number was because our two friends Margaret and Francis lived at Number 18, and he didn't want them worried. Ron stayed with Fred; Fred told Ron there was to be no fuss and no mourning. Fred said he was going to have a good sleep and Ron left saying that he would be in tomorrow.

Ron: After the nurse had shown Dad the book with the correct address, I asked him if he was happy now and he said he was. I am certain that he knew the end was very close and his speech was very difficult to understand, but he was able to say that he did not want to cause any fuss and that there should be no mourning. I stayed with him for quite a while and then he curled up on his side in the foetal position, but he was still struggling to keep awake.

I told him to get a good night's sleep and that I would be in early tomorrow to see him, but I knew deep down that it would be my last visit. I stopped several times as I left the ward to look back and he seemed to be sleeping peacefully. I am absolutely certain that he stayed alive until we returned from holiday and then he allowed himself to just slip away. By the time I got home it must have been about 9.30 p.m. and almost as soon as I had walked into the house, the phone rang, and it was Bryan to say that Dad had passed away.

Mum: The Sister rang Dorothy about 9 o'clock and told her that Fred had passed away. The day nurses and night nurses were with him. The Sister said that we could go within the hour to see him, but Dorothy said we would prefer to remember him as he was when we left him. He told me he loved me and to go home and take some rest. I will always remember my last visit to him, he had a wonderful smile and his face shone and he was smiling. I don't think he saw us go out from the ward as his eyesight had been very poor for some time. Dorothy let Flo and Ron know and it was terrible to think we would never see him again. Fred died on Thursday 30th May 1990 at 9.00 p.m.

On Friday morning Ron and Flo came to Dorothy's and we met up with the undertaker who explained all the arrangements. They then went to the BRI to get Fred's death certificate and then on to register the death. Jean stayed with me at Dorothy's. On the Monday morning Ron took me to Social Services to hand in Fred's pension book and then we went to some insurance offices to let them know and hand in copies of the death certificate.

In the afternoon the Minister from St. Andrew's Church came to see me. The family told the Minister what hymns we would like. He asked me my favourite hymn and I told him: 'One day at a time sweet Jesus'. I asked him not to sing it although it was a great favourite with Fred.

Ron: Mum told me she was afraid that if they played that hymn, she would break down completely.

Mum: On Thursday 6th June 1990 Fred was cremated at Bedminster Down Crematorium. All the families came to my flat first, then when we saw Fred's coffin being driven along Hartcliffe Way the friends and relatives went to the crematorium. Only immediate family followed the hearse. He was cremated at 1.30 p.m. The church was very crowded with friends who had come in coaches and cars. When we got out of the car our Minister was waiting for us. As we followed behind Fred's coffin, I did not realise that they were playing 'One day at a time'. The hymns were lovely, and I watched Fred pass out of sight.

Ron: The weather on the day was dreadful but Mum told me not to worry as 'Happy the bride that the sun shines on and happy the dead that the rain falls on'.

Mum: We all went back to Dorothy's, and they had laid a lovely spread on. Ron and Jean took me back to my own home in the evening and I realised how lonely life was going to be. All my years I have had someone to look after and to look after me. Thank god that I have a loving, caring family to help look after me. I don't worry them, but I know that if I need help they are there to help me. My deepest grief was for Peter in Canada, who could not come over, but the family kept in touch with him by phone and I have spoken to him myself.

After a few weeks without Fred, Jean Reeves of the 'Disabled Club' told me I had to join their club. I go every Monday by coach, and I also go to a Thursday and Friday Club which takes me out of my flat. All the family have been wonderful to me, and they also planned to have a headstone on Fred's grave. We had the headstone put on the grave in May as Fred had been gone a year and you must wait that long before you can do it. It is lovely and we can go to the cemetery and put on flowers. All the family loved the stone and when I go to the cemetery, I feel very close to Fred. He was a wonderful husband and father and if he had lived until 20th July, we would have been married for 60 years.

I go to Dorothy's one weekend, Flo's one weekend and to Ron's the other weekend. I really enjoy my visits and I greatly appreciate all that is done for me by all the families. I have two great grandsons and one great granddaughter, and we enjoy the children's company. I thank God each night for all the help he gives to me. I know I would not last if I didn't have faith and the love of all my family. I have wonderful friends; I love my flat, but I miss Fred so very much. I thank God, however that he is free of pain.

I had a major operation and Fred visited me every day for three weeks and my family used to bring him in to see me and to have him at weekends. We did not realise he was so ill, we thought it was the worry of me until he started with pains in his head and ears. Fred loved his wireless and records. He was very musical but come the last few months he had no interest and just wanted to stay quiet. May God bless all my family including Peter in Canada and, if it is God's will, I would like to live for a long time like my Mum who was 90 when she died.

Ron: These were the last words Mum wrote in answer to the many questions I asked her. I think she knew that she was close to the end. On the last Wednesday that I visited her before 'Black Wednesday' she was in her front room waving her handkerchief out of the top window when I left to go back

*to work. She stayed waving until I went all the way around
the Hartcliffe roundabout and off on the road heading into
Brislington and out of sight.*

I am now going to try to give some more insight into
the twoyears after Dad died but mainly concentrating
on 1992. This was in the main a very bad year for us
and the country.

Martin and Bhebot's marriage was virtually in tat-
ters. Martin rang Nattie and Chris, (Nattie is a lovely
Philippine lady and Bhebot's aunt) to see if they would
come to Clevedon to see if they could help the situation.
They came down and Bhebot said that she was fully com-
mitted to the marriage. Bhebot blamed part of it on hav-
ing to live with us and she wanted her own home.

On that basis we agreed to lend them the deposit money
on a house and eventually with our help they managed
to get a mortgage on a terraced house in Keene's Way,
Clevedon. They moved in with our help and help from
Nattie and Chris on Sunday 1 March 1992: we hoped
that they would start to be happy again. Unfortunately,
this was not to be and within a very short time they
separated.

During my Wednesday visits to Mum, it became obvious
that she was struggling to walk and that her legs were
very swollen. Den had to go into hospital for a prostrate
operation which put additional pressure on Flo. One very
good thing was that Beverly and Trevor were expecting
their first baby and that was brilliant. Hannah was born
on 3 June 1992 in Southmead Hospital.

1992 was the year of the Ebbw Vale Garden Festival which was an attempt to change an old coal site into a beautiful garden show area. There were loads of designer gardens, eco houses, displays, eating places and exhibitions. The plan was to turn this area over to the local population when the show ended. Jean and I had a lovely day there going by paddle steamer from Clevedon Pier across to Penarth and then by coach to Ebbw Vale, passing the Aberfan memorial on the way.

We spent the whole day going around the site and then returned to the boat by about 7.00 p.m. On the way back across the water there was a traditional jazz band and the whole trip was memorable. We were totally exhausted by the time we got home but it was well worth it. The weather continued to be very hot with very little rain. On 25 June 1992 Mum made the same trip with the disabled club. Even though her legs were badly swollen she refused the offer of a wheelchair (she told me she did not want to appear disabled!). It was again very hot, but she walked around the Festival for the whole day. By the time she got back to her flat she was in quite a bad way, and she was ill for several days afterwards.

BLACK WEDNESDAY

Black Wednesday was 16th September 1992, and it is a day that I am never likely to forget. For weeks before that date the financial situation in the UK was becoming dire and every month mortgage rates were going up and up and we were paying about 14 % interest. We were the lucky ones because Jean and I both had good jobs and were able to weather the storm, but many people lost their homes and everything. A new housing estate had been built on the northern outskirts of Bristol and attracted many first-time buyers. The prices of houses plummeted, and many found themselves in negative equity. Bradley Stoke became known as 'sadly broke'.

George Soros was a financial speculator who amazingly made one billion pounds sterling and was dubbed 'the man who broke the Bank of England'. Britain had decided in 1990 to join the European Exchange Rate Mechanism (ERM) which was linked to the euro. British inflation was three times higher than in Germany and speculators anticipated a devaluation of the pound against the Deutshe Mark. During the fortnight leading up to 16 September 1992 speculators sold billions of pounds hoping to buy them back at a depreciated rate and make millions. Among them was George Soros.

On the morning of 16 September, I continually listened to the news as I was driving to work and then I had to make a call on an employee in Portishead. Martin Walker was a technician at the Almondsbury Depot and was suffering from severe depression which had been aggravated by bullying at senior management level at his workplace.

I visited him with Sue Merrell, Senior Personnel Manager from Avon House to agree his ill health retirement package. My plan was to drop Sue back to Avon House, go back to the office in Brislington until lunch time and then do my normal Wednesday visit to Mum.

It was while we were in Portishead that the office got through to Martin Walker's house to say that Mum was very poorly, and an ambulance had been called to take her to the BRI, but they did not know how long the ambulance was going to be. We quickly concluded our meeting, and I dropped Sue off in Bristol before going straight to Mum's.

They were just loading her into the ambulance. Her legs were hugely swollen, and she was in a terrible amount of pain. I followed the ambulance and parked in Park Row before going to reception to find out where they had taken Mum. Lt was very distressing for her because they had put her on a trolley and into a storeroom surrounded by stocks and stores and she was waiting to see a doctor.'

She was in a lot of pain and very scared and all I could do was to stay and hold her hand until the doctor arrived. He was very apologetic about where he had to examine her, but that was the state of the Health Service in 1992 with a severe shortage of beds and huge waiting lists – one of the reasons why Tony Blair swept to power with a massive majority not long afterwards.

After he had examined Mum, he asked me to go outside with him and he explained that the bowel cancer had spread to her kidneys which had become very swollen, and the fluids had gone down into her legs. He said the illness was terminal and that they would find a bed as quickly as possible. I phoned Dot to let her know what was going on and she phoned Flo and they both came in as quickly as possible.

When I got back to Mum, she asked me what the doctor had said and all I could bring myself to say was that they were going to do a series of tests to find out what was wrong. When Dot turned up I left her with Mum and went back to work.

When I got home the financial news was even worse. Interest rates had increased yet again by a further 3 % to 15 % and the Government were predicting even higher interest rates; we were facing a mortgage with close on a 20 % interest rate. Later in the evening the government announced that it was leaving the ERM and reverted to the pegged pound Sterling. Interest rates stabilised around 12 % but a huge amount of damage had been done to the British economy and to individuals at the expense of a few.

I visited Mum during my lunch break on the next day (Thursday) and it was arranged that we would go to see Dr. Habibe the next day (Friday) at noon. Flo came with me and was extremely distressed when Dr. Habibe confirmed that Mum had cancer of the kidneys and how serious the situation was. He said that she would go through a course of treatment but did not seem hopeful of the outcome.

Dot's life was also in turmoil as she was trying to support Mum and then on 18 September 2002 Bryan retired unexpectedly when the company he worked for was taken over and they offered him early retirement, so they would have less money coming in. Recorded in my diary from 18 and 19 September were the following entries including:

Day's going by in a blur. Martin stayed behind at work to celebrate Jim's leaving and got home plastered. Jean and I went shopping for stuff for this weekend's BBQ and Martin took Francia to Bhebot for the weekend. Solicitor's letters about their divorce have now started. We prepared all day on Saturday for our garden BBQ at which 35 Poll Tax Officers attended.

We had a very good evening and we ended up cooking another load of beef burgers at 1.30 in the morning. Denise and Paul stayed the night and then left after we had cooked brunch on Sunday morning (late!). Beverly and Trevor went to the Ebbw Vale Garden Festival, and they dropped off Hannah for us to have for the day. She was extremely good, and we went for a walk up the back lane. The quarry seems to have been stripped of all machinery. France voted very narrowly (49 % to 51 %) to accept the Maastricht Treaty.

I visited Mum again on Monday and was told by the Sister that she would never be able to return home and therefore alternative arrangements would have to be made. Shortly after Dad's first stroke Mum and Dad had a private chat with just me, as they were desperate not to offend anyone. They said that they had carefully discussed their health problems and that they knew that things could get worse. They both emphasised strongly that they did not wish, either together or individually' to come to live with any of the family.

They said that they had seen this happen many times before and that it never worked out and would only cause their family heartache. They were totally adamant about this and had obviously thought about it a lot and had agreed this between themselves.

I went into work very early on 22 September and had my first meeting at 7.45 a.m. I then went into the BRI to see Graham Mackintosh, a social worker at 12.45 p.m. It was obvious that they wanted to get her out of hospital and into a residential home. Mum seemed quite cheerful even though she now knew that she had cancer; probably all a front because she did not want us upset.

We went out for a meal in the evening to the Bridge Inn with Linda, Rose, Martin and Francia but it is very difficult to relax and enjoy ourselves. On 23 September when I went in to see her, Mum was very low, extremely tired, and very confused: I felt so dreadfully sorry for her. On 24 September Jean, Martin and I visited Mum straight from work, and she was much better, more composed, and able to hold her own cup etc. After the visit Jean and I went to Lily and Eric's for advice on what we should look for in choosing a nursing home. Lily was very helpful and then she said that from her experience as a nurse dealing with terminally ill patients, Mum had possibly four to six months to live.

As soon as we got home, I rang Peter in Canada to update him on the news and he said that he would try to get over for Mum's birthday. Martin broke the news to Bhebot who apparently was very upset and broke down in tears.

Went in to see Mum on 25th and got the news that Peter had rung Flo to say he was coming over on the 10 October. On the 26th we went in with Martin and Francia but Mum was very weak and looking very frail. Had another chat with the Sister and they are saying that she will have to vacate the bed soon. She is unable to go home and yet she needs 24-hour care and because we all work, none of us can look after her.

On Sunday 27th September Jean and I went to visit a nursing home in Clifton. We were not that impressed; the room was very small but did have a window looking out over the garden. The staff and patients seem very friendly, but the room is on the first floor right opposite the top of the stairs which looked a hazard. This might be the best available in the short term as there is a severe shortage of good accommodation.

On 28th I visited Mum on my own during the lunch hour. She was very poorly and was being very sick which could be a reaction to the drugs they keep pumping into her. On the 29th Martin went in to see her and later Bhebot visited her separately. When we saw her she was a little better, but her colostomy bag is not clearing properly. I spoke to Dot and Flo, and everyone is feeling exhausted with the stress and the constant running around.

On 30th I visited her again during the lunch hour and Debra was there with her friend Corrie. Mum was very poorly indeed, and we hope that she will live until Peter arrives from Canada.

The next couple of days were spent rushing around trying to arrange things before we went off to Butlin's at Bognor Regis for a long weekend with Martin and Francia and visiting Mum. I went all the way to Hartcliffe to try to get her pension money that she had asked me to collect, only to find that the post office was closed, and then I got caught in an horrendous traffic jam as they were resurfacing the main Well's Road – nothing was going right.

On Saturday 3 October after visiting, we went to Flo and Den's to sort out the financial arrangements and our contributions to Mum's stay in the nursing home. It is no use hiding that this was going to be a huge financial struggle for all of us. Bryan was now on a pension and Dennis's health was not that good. We all had mortgages, and the repayments were escalating at a worrying rate. We were all dreading putting her into a home, and Jean and I discussed having her stay with us as we have the largest house, although it would mean Jean going back to job-share again.

On Sunday 4 October Jean, Martin and I went in again and stayed for over two hours. Mum was finding it extremely difficult to speak, was extremely tired and looked like a skeleton. I went to see the Ward Sister on my own and told her in no uncertain terms that they must keep mum in hospital and not send her to the nursing home because she was very seriously ill. The ward Sister promised me that she would see what she could do.

I spoke to Dorothy and Flo again to see whether we should cancel our long weekend in Bognor Regis, but they both agreed that we should go ahead but keep in contact. Beverly was not coming with us and so would be the 'go-between'. I did not think at that time what Mum's realistic life expectancy was and was somewhat guided by Lily's advice.

On Monday 5 October we had a good trip down to Bognor Regis, stopping off for lunch as we could not get into our accommodation until 4.00 p.m. We had a living room, two bedrooms, kitchen, and shower room all in nice condition. In the evening we went to a show to see Stan Boardman who was very funny and kept talking about the 'Jairmans' (Germans). We went to the 'Captain's table' before the show, but the meal was very poor. It was dry but cold and we were able to walk around the site to see the various events taking place.

I rang Beverly in the evening, and she told me that Mum could now stay in the hospital and would not have to go into the nursing home. This was a tremendous relief. She also said that she had taken Hannah in so that Mum could see her but had been told off by the nurse for taking a baby into the hospital – Mum would have wanted to see her new great grandchild, so they were way out of order.

She also said that Trevor had taken our beautiful ginger (female) cat to the vets (she had been poorly for a couple of days) and they had to put her down because she was suffering from kidney failure. Yet more bad news.

We had Suki from the time she was a kitten and we bought her from the dogs' home in Brislington; the same place we had bought Bengi from. She had quickly established her place in the home after initially we kept Bengi downstairs and Suki upstairs. It was obvious that this arrangement could not continue and so eventually we brought them together. In the end they would sleep in the same basket together. She was about 18 years old when she died.

Bengi had been put to sleep about a year earlier on 6 February 1991 at about 17 years old after suffering badly from arthritis, a common complaint with Benji's type of dog which was a cross between Labrador and Doberman.

On Tuesday 6 October 1992 we went swimming in the huge water complex and went down the 'Black hole' which was very scary. In the afternoon we saw a show in the theatre called 'Grease Lightning' all about rock and roll and that was also very good. I rang Beverly before going into see 'Jerry and the Pacemakers' and she said that Mum was very poorly.

At about 6.45 a.m. on Wednesday morning the security guard knocked on our door and got me out of bed. He asked me to ring Trevor who told me that Mum's condition had deteriorated, and her breathing was very shallow. Dot and Flo went straight in to see her, and I then spoke to Dot who gave me the number of the doctor to ring.

I spoke to the doctor and asked whether we should come home, but he said that they were changing her drugs to try to stabilise her and that there was no way in which I could help. Had it been just Jean and I then we would have returned immediately, but we had Martin and Francia with us and it did not seem fair if there was nothing we could do – agonising decisions.

We decided to take Francia on a train ride and so we took the short trip into the centre of Bognor Regis. It is a sleepy little seaside town with nothing much to see so we had lunch in a McDonald's and then returned to camp. Beverly rang shortly afterwards to say that Mum had passed away at 5.20 p.m. 7 October 1992.

Dorothy and Flo were both with her when she died, and they found it a dreadful experience. I spoke at length to Dennis who said that there was even less sense to return home now and that they would continue with the funeral arrangements and that we would all meet up at Dot and Bryan's on Friday evening.

On Thursday morning we went into Portsmouth and Martin and Francia had a good time. We had an extremely good lunch in a pub that catered for children and then went back to the site. Martin took Francia to watch the donkey races and I went for a long walk to get my thoughts together. Jean stayed in the chalet because she was 'miffed' that we had not done all the shops in Bognor! In the evening we went to see a version of 'It's a knockout' which was very entertaining. The holiday was not as carefree as it should have been because of the circumstances, but the accommodation and entertainment was excellent although the quality of the food was poor.

On Friday morning we had breakfast and then set off early for home. We got home about 1.00 p.m. and in the evening went to Dot and Bryan's to confirm the funeral arrangements. Peter had just arrived from Canada, and it was so sad that he was too late to see Mum before she died. Perhaps it was better for him to remember her as he last saw her – who can tell?

In recent months there had been stories of people arguing over the deceased's possessions even before the funeral had taken place, and this had caused major family rows. We all agreed that this was the last thing Mum would have wanted to happen, and so we all agreed not to even discuss her possessions until after the funeral.

The funeral took place on Tuesday 13th October 1992, and we all went to her home at 34 Waldegrave House, Hartcliffe, Bristol. We all got there before 11.a.m. The funeral cars turned up promptly at 11.40 a.m. and we then followed it to Bristol Crematorium on Bedminster Down, where Dad had been cremated and buried just two years earlier.

We quickly noticed that the cross of flowers that we had ordered as a family for placing on top of the coffin was not there, and it later transpired that the Funeral Director had forgotten to order it. Little things like this can cause huge significance for people who are exhausted and down.

The weather was beautiful all day which made things easier, and it was a very nice and compassionate service carried out by the Reverend Francis. Afterwards we all went back to Dorothy's for the afternoon and then in the evening Jean and I went out for a meal on our own. Martin did not come as Francia was being grumpy and so he got himself fish and chips.

After the funeral Mr Gare of Thomas Davis the undertakers agreed that his company would donate £60 to St. Peter's Hospice in recognition of his firm's failure to provide the cross as ordered. We had agreed that any compensation should go to that charity as none of us wanted to profit by someone else's mistake.

The Council only allow you a very short time to clear out the flat so that they can re-let it and so on Thursday 15 October we all met up at Mum's flat to sort out her possessions. This went very well, and we came to agreement very quickly. Flo was looking very strained, and the shock seemed suddenly to have caught up with Bryan, but Dorothy was coping very well.

We had the glass oak cabinet which Mum had asked me to take because I had promised to get the two damaged panes of glass mended, and a small square table. Dorothy had some jewellery, the pouffe and the TV cabinet. Flo had jewellery, the two small Japanese vases, and the writing bureau. Philip had the dining room table and chairs. Carol had the dressing table and Richard had the bed, wardrobe, black and white television and any other bits and pieces left over as he was furnishing his house.

When Trevor and I went in his van to collect the glass cabinet, all the joints had dried out in the central heating and the complete bottom part fell to pieces making it very hard to move. We all agreed that Peter could pick the items from the glass cabinet and any photographs and other small sentimental items that he could take back with him on the plane.

I gave Dot a copy of Mum's memoirs, and she was going to get it edited and typed up, but she has recently told me that she could not bear to read it. Just to complicate matters Francia went down with Chicken Pox and was quite poorly for a while. However, it is said that it is better to have Chicken Pox while you are young, than later in life.

Life was getting ever tougher as Margaret Thatcher announced another round of pit closures with the loss of a further 30,000 jobs and Arthur Scargill was beginning to flex his muscles (although it must be said that a lot of people were very uneasy about the government's actions as it was clear that they were gearing up for a fight to the death, having stockpiled millions of tons of coal). It must also be remembered that the miners were responsible for the Conservatives' humiliation and subsequent resignation of Prime Minister Ted Heath when he went to the country for backing against the miners and did not get it.

On 3 November 1992 Martin's divorce from Bhebot became 'absolute' and we could not comprehend how everything had happened so quickly. Martin walked away from the marriage with absolutely nothing as he wanted Francia to have a nice house to be brought up in. I decided that in memory of Mum and Dad I would have their glass cabinet repaired quickly as the panes of glass had been broken for as long as I can remember.

The glass edges are curved and in delicate surroundings, but I managed to find a glazier in Sandy Park Road, Brislington, Bristol who was willing to tackle the job. He completed it before the end of the year, but he confessed that it was the most nerve-racking job he had ever tackled.

Local government was facing severe cutbacks with rumours that over 4,000 people were to be made redundant. The year seemed to be going from bad to worse and then we had a phone from Mrs Protestante asking us to let Bhebot know that her dad was seriously ill. Martin had his car broken into and the rats even stole the child's seat.

Then things slowly started to improve and on 4 December 1992 we went to Dot and Bryan's retirement party at the Parkway Tavern in Filton and over 100 friends and relatives turned up. It was a lovely evening after such a sad year, made even better when they announced that Debra is expecting her first child.

On 17 December Martin was appointed to Senior Officer Grade in the Recovery Section with a massive salary increase of almost £5,000 and essential car user status. On 21 December Martin rang his friends Paul and Mercia (they spent a lot of time together as two couples while stationed in Germany) to wish them happy Christmas. He learned from them that Bhebot was seven months' pregnant with Clive's baby. Clive and Bhebot got married not long after and then divorced. So ended 1992 and this is where I am going to end Mum's story.

My summing up of 1992 as recorded in my diary reads as follows;

What can I say about 1992? Probably one of the most difficult years for everyone throughout the country full of tensions and anxieties, wars and conflicts every single day. Martin got divorced but even this was overshadowed by Mum's death which happened very suddenly and has still not really sunk in. I still cannot get use to not having our Wednesday meetups and Sunday chats or visits.

Hannah was born and is a lovely baby and Francia has grown up a lot although she is not as well behaved as we would like.

We had to have Suki put to sleep and so for the first time for many years we have no pets. We spend a lot of money feeding the wild birds which is lovely. We learnt that Bhebot was seven months' pregnant, and that Clive (Dangerfield) is the father.

Jean and I had a reasonably 'fight free' year although unfortunately we ended up the old year/started the New Year on bad terms. Martin has recovered well from his divorce and is rebuilding his life again.

Ron Brooks
27 January 2023

Arthur Croome

Arthurs's War: Arthur Croome

2 March 1923 – 26 December 2004

Grandad, you know that I am now eleven,
and grown up, Francia said
And there is something that has been going,
around in my head
You speak fondly of your sisters, your brother,
your aunts, and your uncles
But I have not met many of them,
and that causes me troubles

I pondered on this and thought, she is absolutely right
And it troubled me as I tried to sleep in the night
I must do something to solve her obvious despair
And I must do it quickly, to show that I care

So, I sent invitations to every one of my relatives
And to those few of Jeanette's,
who had not emigrated abroad
But the response was disappointing,
many had previous engagements
Try again, but give plenty of notice this time,
by Jeanette, was what I was told

I pondered on this, and the conditions required
Not during the school holidays that would not be desired
Away from the cold, the snow, and the rain
Where we could barbeque outside, without any pain

So, for the first Sunday in June, I sent an annual invitation
Relief from the winter cold, the wet and sun deprivation
Relatives could book it for many years ahead
That's a very good idea, young Francia said

And so that has been the pattern, for a great many years
Although for some times, death caused a number of tears
But overall, it was a truly marvellous success
And everyone mucked in, to save extra stress

But I must tell you of the reunion that gave
a surprise to us all
It was Sunday June 1, 2003
The weather was stunning, the garden and scenery,
left people in awe
A brilliant turnout, and a wonderful spree

We men were all standing (or lounging)
around under the pergola,
I was cooking the barbeque, the others:
doing nothing in particular
Sausages, beefburgers, chicken legs,
and chicken breast, all on the flames
Everyone drinking, chewing the fat,
telling stories and planning some games

The women were gathered in the kitchen, preparing
starters and puddings
I bet the men are up there talking about women, food,
cricket, and other shenanigans
Cooking the food on the BBQ is a manly job, they think
They would be so much more useful,
with their hands in the sink!

But this time it was different, the subject:
a very different persuasion
Next year would be 60 years since '
D' Day, and the Normandy invasion
Commemorations were being planned, all around the world
Memories came flooding back as the stories unfold

Uncle Bill regaled us of his time in Egypt,
sand up to where it irritates most!
I asked him if my long promised camel had escaped,
or was still travelling, here in the post!
Bryan was describing his skiing in Austria,
his extremities trying to be kept as warm as toast
And how he had been offered a job as ski trainer,
by his very amiable Austrian host
Vern declined to answer questions about
his time in a German POW camp
Other than to say that the British Red Cross saved his life
And enabled him to get back to his beloved old Blighty
And for him to make Aunty Vi, his wonderful wife

Arthur, surprisingly, had little to say about
his time in Germany
He spoke more of Iris, who now also was his wife
They had been together since kids at school in Horfield
She stuck by him, and is obviously, the love of his life

We talked about Stan who had died quite young
And we knew of his posting to Cyprus, out there in the sun
I revealed that his best mate was killed in an ambush
Sat next to him as their lorry, by a terrorist group,
was rushed

Stan was just eleven years older than me
And I was often in trouble with my sisters as
he and I went on a spree
They thought he was a bad influence,
on my upbringing
But he was a joy to be with: an awful lot of grinning!

Dennis said he was jealous of their worldly escapades
He had been stuck in Catterick Camp,
for his entire service days
Just counting down the time to demob: day by day
Unable to get home to see Florence, a great distance away.

At that moment Iris came up from the kitchen
She stopped for a moment listening what was being said
Can you stop your jabbering, and your bitching?
My stomach thinks that my mouth has been sewn up
and I need to be fed

Oh, and has Arthur told you that we have been invited
To the 60 year commemorations of 'D' Day next year
We are hoping to return to Gold Beach: we are so excited
And then on to the Netherlands: totally delighted.

Puzzled looks came across everyone of our faces
What do you mean: return to Gold Beach, why are you going?
When were you first there? Just what were you doing?
Arthur, I hope you weren't there, just those young
girls a wooing!

Hi, look guys, I've already told you, my stomach
thinks my throat's cut
Iris said a little tetchily, but with a twinkle in her eye
Arthur is a hero, he landed there on 'D' Day
Now pick up the food and follow me this way,
before from hunger I die

It was a moment of amazement; this had not been planned
One by one we stood up, and solemnly shook his hand
We had better do what Iris says, do what we are told
But after we have eaten, your adventures, you must unfold

A bevy of drinks and some fabulous food
Soon put us in a relaxed and garrulous mood
So come on Arthur, just spill the beans
We are astounded; amazed, you are clearly, not what you seem

But I just saw no reason to talk about it,
was Arthur's opening line
I was just joining my relatives and friends in the fight
It was nothing heroic, I was just doing my duty,
doing my time
We hoped that Operation Overlord would
destroy Hitler, and all of his might

Our second battalion of the Glosters sailed
from Portsmouth, one day later than expected
The weather had been atrocious; but then it relented
That journey across the Channel, scared us all to death
And as we approached the beaches, a cacophony
of noise from the guns, made us totally deaf

On Tuesday 6 June 1944 at 11:00am,
our Normandy beach landings relentlessly began
We were the second wave to land at Gold Beach,
slowly, nervously, just man by man
Once ashore, loaded with equipment,
as fast as possible, we dashed up the beach
Desperate to stay alive until the relative safety
of cover, we finally reached.

They say a cat has nine lives, Arthur said with a laugh
My first I almost lost when exiting the beach landing craft
I stepped off into the water:
must have been over six feet deep
My comrades pulled me gasping, ashore: I still relive
the moment, the fear, every night in my sleep.

My job then was to drive a Bren gun carrier, through
France and through Belgium
The dates and places are etched deep in my brain
We battled fiercely, heroically, overcoming the fear
and hardship, just begun
We would not give up until we reached our target;
the incredibly important, the River Seine

We joined up with different units and slowly pushed east
By the eleventh of June, Tilly-sur-Seulles under
Operation Perch had been reached
On 30 July under Operation Bluecoat,
the Saint-Germain d'Ectot ridge
Then by 12 August Thury-Harcourt under
Operation Tractable: taken, ditch by ditch.

And then on 25 August a major, bruising,
destructive, engagement
At Épaignes some of the fiercest street
by street fighting, of that vicious war
Me, the invincible, was one of the 53 casualties
The second of my nine lives was used: That's for sure!

A sniper bullet hit my helmet and knocked me flat
on my back,
A long crease was made in that safety steel hat
I was knocked unconscious, but my courageous
mates pulled me through
Without the selflessness of comrades in battle;
just what would we do!

Other than a splitting fierce headache for a number of days
I was able to resume my duties, and we went on our ways
And on second of September, we crossed the River Rouen
But we were getting further and further,
away from our home

We spearheaded the assault on Le Havre on
the tenth of September
Two days later, we were the first to enter
and captured their fort,
Together with 1,500 prisoners and more beer
than we could drink
But the fact that forty of our comrades were killed
or were injured; made our hearts sink
From Le Havre, our Battalion advanced into Belgium,
Seeing action in the bridgehead across
the Turnhout-Antwerp Canal,
And then into the Netherlands,
where at Stampersgat we battled
The Dutch people, battered and shattered:
living in hell

Among the casualties was our battalion commander,
Lieutenant-Colonel Francis Butterworth,
He died of wounds received during the attack
at Stampersgat on 6 November 1944,
Here we had all battled for all of our worth:
a truly brutal and terrible day
He was immediately succeeded by the very
experienced, Lieutenant-Colonel Robert Gray
Despite our setbacks we had no option, but to push on,
relentlessly, with the fight
Travelling in all weathers, over all landscapes,
by day and by night
But slowly and surely although our progress seemed slow
One by one we defeated them, and overcame the foe
It was heart-warming as we liberated,
each village after village
The joy in their eyes, the relief on their faces,
made our sacrifices worthwhile
Getting angrier and angrier as we learnt of the killing,
the rape and the pillage
People everywhere literally starving to death;
the treatment of the Jews, absolutely vile

We reached Nijmegen in late November; the weather
now autumnal and not very pleasant
We advanced slowly and cautiously to avoid further casualties
But the Germans were getting increasingly more
and more desperate
And Hitler, in a final desperate fling,
used his best troops on an entirely different strategy

And so, on 16 December the 'Battle of the Bulge' began
This tested the Americans to their very last man
German troops broke through the Ardennes Forest
in Belgium and Luxembourg
Causing mayhem: the Americans unable to send
in air relief because of the weather

The Germans were desperate knowing they
were facing defeat
And so, they were fanatical using suicidal feats
The fighting was brutal, ferocious, barring no holds
And as winter encroached, they were faced
with a deep bitter, winter cold
Then for a short time in Holland, the fighting subsided
But now, we were all battling the intense cold,
terror, and hunger
Many soldiers suffered sickness, fever and shell shock,
Dutch civilians were forced to live underground,
without any stock.

The daily life of the 3.5 million Dutch people living
in still-occupied parts of Holland
Was dominated by a relentless and increasingly des-
perate search for supplies
The Germans were vicious;
executions common for minor demeanours
As a result of this 'Hunger Winter',
around 20,000 Dutch people died.
In late January as the weather started
to improve on the Bulge
The Yanks sent in reinforcements: more men,
more ammunition, more food
This turned the tide, and the Jerries were
forced to retreat,
And by 25 January, 1945, they all knew they were beat

It was the largest, bloodiest single battle fought
by the US in World War Two
They suffered 89,000 casualties, 19,000 killed:
of the Germans nobody knew
It was the final death knell for Germany,
Berlin was in sight
And from the East came the Russians to get revenge,
and to worsen Germany's plight
That hard fought victory allowed us to move
towards the Rhine.
And the continued liberation of Holland's cities,
towns and villages: one at a time

Our last major battle came on 12 April, when we
crossed the River Ijssel at Arnhem,
And to everyone's relief we captured the town,
and the Germans: we disarmed them!
The Germans surrender on the seventh day of May,
But it was not until the next day it effectively took place
The feeling of relief and euphoria is hard to describe
And I have never been kissed by so many girls in my life!
We entered Germany near Osnabrück and
moved on to Berlin
The place just rubble, the people scared, injured and thin
It was very hard to feel sorry,
after through all that we had been
And the horrors we were learning about,
ghastly, scene after scene

Our battalion provided a detachment of guards
at the Nuremberg trials
And at one stage I was stationed outside the cell
of the Nazi, Rudolph Hess
At least, he had tried to make peace by flying
to Scotland
And perhaps when he finally committed suicide,
it was all for the best.

And then Arthur just said simply: well,
that was my war
A lot of people did the same, and many,
very much more
The bonus was that all of our relatives finally
got home alive
Because during many long harrowing days,
I thought none would survive

There was a moment of silence, then clapping and cheers
And this very humble man fought hard,
to keep back the tears
But they gave us a full month's holiday, with service's pay
And then straight back to work with SWEB,
the following day

Between the Normandy landings,
Victory in Europe and the horrors of war
Our battalion suffered 700 casualties:
injured or killed, and perhaps many more
On 4 May each year, Holland commemorates
Remembrance Day a tribute to the injured or killed.
And 5 May, is Liberation Day where,
never to be forgotten promises, are solemnly fulfilled

On 22 September, 1951, Arthur finally got to marry
Iris, his sweetheart, in church.
They had been courting since the start of the war,
and she never left him in the lurch
The marriage delayed because of her serious health illnesses
It was Arthur's turn to stay true,
and to honour his promises

The wedding itself was a joyous affair
A huge family turnout and no expense was spared
It was first time I had gone to a fully laid out reception
White table clothes, silver cutlery, wonderful food:
it was perfection

Drink was in abundance, and our first introduction to wine
For my sisters, aged 18 and 19, this was sublime
My sister Florence got very drunk, without even knowing
But that is the subject of a very different poem

Sadly, because of her illness,
Iris was instructed not to have children
A great disappointment because large families
were the norm
But for us two young boys, it was heaven indeed
As they were both extremely generous in
helping supply our family needs

Just look below at the wedding photograph,
and Arthurs's very smart suit
When I started work just three years later,
the family did not have much loot
Iris said: 'Ron is nearly as tall as Arthur now,
but not quite his size
He can have his wedding suit;
he might have to beef up a bit: especially his thighs!'

All my aunts, uncles, sisters and brother and parents of bride and groom at the wedding. I am in short pants, front row, closest to the bridesmaid. Note the sharp creases in the short pants!

So, I started work looking, like the bee's knees
Not having to wear ragged clothes, so no one could tease
Just another example of their thoughtfulness,
loving and caring
And to be able to help us, they had no problems sharing

At Christmas, our presents were always generous,
and thoughtful
And Christmas 1952, for my brother and I,
an autograph book
And for one year in 1953 I was a 'stage door Johnny',
Please give me your autograph:
I said with a pleading look.

Frank Sinatra does not give autographs,
the doorman advised
But he stopped for us, to everyone's surprise
With Julie Andrews I ended up chasing her
right down the street
The doorman pointing her out because
I did not recognise her: you'd better be fleet!

Every Tuesday at our house,
the four adults would play cards
Whist or Rummy, Cribbage, Poker, Patience or Hearts
Often I would creep down the stairs to hear what was said
We know you are there Ron, now get back to bed!

After every game's session they had a repast
The supply of food was now getting slightly easier, at last
Buttered Jacobs cream crackers, and real Cheddar cheese
With Mum's own pickled onions, and gallons of tea.

My one abiding memory of the fun that,
on one day they had,
Was Arthur on the floor being tickled by Mum
and by Iris, urged on by my Dad
They just wouldn't stop, no matter how much he protested
Until finally it was too much, he got quite mad,
his patience severely tested

But sadly, Arthur never made those 60th celebrations
A vicious cruel stroke struck him down,
and stopped their intentions
His speech, arms and legs all seriously affected
What would his life be like now, we sadly reflected?

The last time I saw Arthur was at the funeral
of my Aunty Vi: January 2004
Entering hospital for a minor operation,
as a spritely 87 year old
She contracted the infection sepsis,
whilst recovering in there
My cousins were never able to establish the real facts:
that was really unfair.

I remember Arthur being helped out of the funeral car
And with the support of myself and Iris,
we got him through the crematorium door
A shadow of the man, it was pitiful to see
But he was determined to give his older sister
a send-off: that was him to a tee

Arthur made it to Boxing Day, that very same year
Offered a full military funeral,
Iris did not want all that fuss
Instead, eight veterans from the Gloster Regiment
formed a guard of honour
And proudly stood over him, until he was lowered

Iris: beautiful, elegant, proud, all dressed in black
Walked solemnly on her own, behind the cortege
A fitting end for a wonderful man,
from his wonderful wife
And I shall do my best to emulate him,
for the rest of my life

The wake, once the great sadness had eased,
was amazing
The Veterans from the Glosters Regiment,
superbly entertaining
Story after story, one after another, joyously regaling
And their love for their comrade: totally compelling

I visited Iris until her very difficult decision was made
To move closer to her family, north of Whitchurch way
To be lovingly supported by her family,
her sister and her brother
And at 93 years old, she slowly and peacefully slipped away

She was the last of my aunties and uncles
and it was a very sad day
And now I just hold onto my memories,
and cannot say much more
That generation which spanned those terrible
two great wars
I admire unreservedly, and there was not a single
one of them, that I did not adore

I feel a deep sense of gratitude to my Grandmas
and Grandads
Who brought up all their children in an impeccable way,
Through hard times and good times, happy times
and sad times
Differences of opinions, in different times,
sorted and with love, usually swept away

For those of the younger generation and those who do not know my family, here is a brief history of those involved in this poem:

My Mum:
- Emily Catherine Florence Brooks (nee Croome) born 22 October 1909. Died 7 October 1992. Always known as Em or Emmy

Mum's siblings:
- Florence Lilian Catley (nee Croome – Aunty Flo): born 2 April 1913. Died 2 April 2005
- James William Croome (Uncle Bill): born 1 September 1915. Died 3 March 1993
- Violet St. Clair (nee Croome – Aunty Vi): born 29 April 1917. Died 16 January 2004
- Arthur Croome (Uncle Arthur): born 2 March 1923. Died 26 December 2004
- Stanley Ronald Croome (Uncle Stan): born 12 May 1927. Died 23 May 1978

Iris Croome (nee Shaw – Aunty Iris):
- born 5 May 1926. Died 20 August 2019

My Dad:
- Albert Frederick Brooks (Fred) born 9 January 1909. Died 30 May 1990

Dad's siblings:

- Mary Anne Rowe Brooks (nicknamed Polly) born 7 December 1905. Died 30 March 1974
- Lily Rose Brooks born 31 January 1907. Died of heart problems 29 August 1927. Broke my Dad's heart.
- Gladys May Brooks born 13 April 1924 (same day and month as my brother Peter). Died 7 September 2017

My sisters:

- Dorothy Lilian Greenhill (nee Brooks – Dot) born 13 January 1933
- Florence Mary Porter (nee Brooks – Flo) born 13 January 1934

Dot and Flo were born exactly one year apart because my Mum was told by her mother that you could not get pregnant while you were breast feeding. Like many old wives tales: Wrong!

Me:

- Ronald Frederick Brooks (Ron) born 14 November 1938

My brother:

- Peter William Brooks (Pete) born Easter Sunday 13 April 1941

Mum gave birth to Peter during the Easter bombings in Bristol, and we were a mile from Filton Airfield, a prominent target. During that weekend three houses were completely destroyed about 400 yards away from us, and our windows were blown in and our ceilings collapsed.

And finally, a nice picture of Uncle Arthur, Uncle Vern, Aunty Iris and Aunty Vi.

Operation Overlord – Gold Beach
2nd Battalion Gloucestershire Regiment

Front and Back of medal

Ron Brooks
1 December 2021

Korean War – The forgotten War:
25 June 1950 to 27 July 1953

Our square-bashing and training
at Bullwell Barracks had finished
Our Passing Out parade had gone exactly to plan
We stood there expectantly, waiting for our postings
Making light of it but, really, all scared to a man.

What that envelope revealed would determine our future
A cushy safe posting or a terrifying war zone
Soon to be off on our adventures, to distant horizons
We had just two weeks on leave before departing
from home

I opened my envelope and stared in amazement
I was going to Austria, to learn how to ski
Patrolling the borders against terrorist insurgents,
Doing my bit to keep Europe safe, and enemy free

My best mate Buster, looked at his posting, and chuckled
I'm off overseas to Korea, for lots of sunshine and thrills
Although to be honest I don't know the heck
where it's located
I just hope it is populated by attractive young girls.

It's right next to China I knowingly informed him
And those Eastern girls are gorgeous beauties to behold
But you'd better keep your pants up,
and shirt well and truly buckled as
Easterners are very possessive of their women,
or so I am told

I know all about those Geezer girls,
Buster knowingly opined
And from what I have heard, they are loving,
intelligent, loyal and kind
I think you mean Geisha girls, I laughingly corrected
And they are Japanese not Chinese,
and seriously protected

I did not like to tell Buster the grim situation
I had heard on the wireless in the NAAFI last night
North Korea had crossed the 38th Parallel
Invaded the south: I knew we were in for a right
royal fight

A dozen years later I was walking through Broadmead,
From Dunn's in the High Street, at the end of my day
When a tap on my shoulder, stopped me in full speed
'How be you, me mucker?' I heard someone say.

Bryan, I'd recognise you anywhere,
you haven't changed a bit
Even though back then we were youngsters,
and both very fit
What are you up to, and how has life treated you?
I would love for our friendship, now to continue

I recognised the voice and so stopped, and turned round
This wizened, dishevelled, grey haired old man,
just stood his ground
For a moment I stood there, who could this guy be?
Surely not Buster, can't be: he's the same age as me?

I recovered my composure and heard myself say
I'm just going for a snifter to wind down my day
So why don't you come with me to the old Phoenix pub
And if you are hungry, I will buy you some grub.

We sat at our table waiting for our beef pie and chips
He was shaking all over, a fag between his lips
I could not believe this was Buster,
my friend and best mate
The fun loving joker, with not a single ounce of hate

I studied him carefully, and then broke the ice
I wanted to be careful and to say something funny,
but also nice
The last time I saw you was at Bullwell training barracks
Where the menu back then, was boiled beef and carrots!

He sat looking down for a moment, and then gravely said
'After everything that I've been through,
it's a surprise I'm not dead.'
Our 1st Battalion of the Glorious Glosters was split into two
Of those selected to go into my section,
the survivors are few.

The first thing that happened:
National Service was extended
A long eighteen months was what had been intended
Then Government decided: two years was the need
Ironically, it did not affect me: I was in a POW camp:
waiting to be freed.

I tried to lighten the mood by saying:
My Dot was incandescent
Our nuptials she had been planning for months;
and our presents!
We were forced to put back the date of our
much vaunted event
And for me: in my tax rebate a very serious dent!

Bryan, you were so lucky to go to Austria,
to have fun in the snow
To visit Vienna, and interesting places
that you got to know
In October 1950 our 1st Battalion of the
Gloucestershire Regiment
Sailed from Southampton, and on saving South Korea,
we were hell bent

The Band of the Gloster Regiment stood
proudly on the quayside
And played 'Far away places' as we sailed out to sea
Leaving behind, our family our friends and
many others beside,
We hoped to save the world from a possible, terrible,
destructive, World War Three

A welcome respite on a slow boat to Korea
Aboard HMT Empire Windrush, a luxury passenger liner
Taken as reparations for Germany's misdemeanours
We could not have travelled on anything finer!

Buster's shakes reminded me of a customer,
in the 'Hole in the Wall'
Who jokingly told people his name was
Arthur Sidney Hole,
His real name was Leslie but that would not raise laugh
From those sat around the bar, drinking their pints of
George's draught

Les suffered badly from shell shock,
trapped at the war front on the Somme
He would shake and hold his wrist down to write
and be calm
Watching him struggle to compose himself,
was a terrible sight
But he could hold a pint without spilling a drop: no
sign there of his plight!

Buster continued: The first part of the battle
was a bit of a doddle
The Yanks had pushed the enemy back over the line
Our regiment had captured Hill 327 with no
or little trouble
We then sat there as observers: just biding our time

And then Chinese and Russian reinforcements
came to the aid of the foe
And under great pressure and bombardment,
we had nowhere to go
Our options were limited, forced to retreat
back to Hill 235
And we started to wonder:
Would escape with our lives?

The 63rd Chinese infantry waded across the Imjin
River, on the night of 22 April 1951,
We fiercely repelled them, for not one,
not two, but three days or more
Time was a blur and then totally surrounded,
what of the reinforcements: absolutely none
We were outnumbered, out fought, out manoeuvred,
beaten: and finally done!

All our ammunition, strength,
courage and energy was spent
Our battle to save the world from communism:
a lost event
I lost conscious as a bullet, struck me in my left chest
My life saved by a purloined, American,
body-armoured vest

Shell shocked and shaken we surrendered to the enemy
Bloodied and beaten, many injured or dead
Licking our wounds, this was never foreseen or imagined
Brutally and humiliated, all I wanted to do,
was to lay on my bed.

But they forced us to take the long walk to the
prison of war camps
Walking long weary hours, both by day and by night
We trudged over endless mountains,
marched through forests, forded freezing rivers.
By the time we arrived, those of us that survived,
were a terrible sight.

Over two long years we were prisoners of war
And the starvation and the dreadful conditions
have taken their toll
Endlessly browbeaten in a bid to convert
us to communism
It was loyalty to my country that kept me strong:
this was not heroism

But let me remind you, Bryan, my friend
Our Glosters motto is 'By our deeds we are known'
In a hundred years' time people will look back and say
Those Gloster lads were amazing,
on such days' liberty is sown

Tears streamed down my cheeks as he related his story
Of his sufferings, whilst I was having a jolly good time
My guilt was unbearable, inconsolable, without any glory
I just grasped hold of his hand and said:
'I'm sure you'll be fine.'

It was deeply inadequate; I knew that full well,
And I hoped he would get better, but only time would tell
My life changed completely that very sad day
And I just didn't know what to say to him,
as he slowly walked away.

Outside the pub we had said our goodbyes
I have no permanent address yet, he said with a sigh
But keep your chin up me babby,
everything will be all right
And with that he disappeared, shuffling into the night

I should have been there to help you, through your ordeal
Can you imagine for one moment,
how that makes me feel?
I just hoped that he could have a really good life
Free of worries, anxiety and undeserved strife

But sadly, like many who served their country
with pride
He thought that his only way out,
was to put an end to his life
His demons controlled him and forced him,
without a doubt
To commit suicide: no future, no hope:
his only way out.

Just a few facts that I would like anyone who reads this poem to know

More than 700 Glosters fought in the brutal and bloody Battle of Imjin. 59 soldiers of the Gloucestershire Regiment were killed in action. 522 soldiers of the Gloucestershire Regiment became prisoners of war. Of those taken prisoner, 180 were wounded and a further 34 died while in captivity.

The people of Korea have never forgotten the debt they owe to the men who fought for their liberty. Korean War veterans are welcomed whenever they visit South Korea. Hill 235 is now officially named 'Gloster Hill'.

The Korean War has never officially ended. Skirmishes still occur along the border, which remains the most heavily militarised frontier in the world. Today, North Korea is an isolated communist state. South Korea is a democracy with a burgeoning economy. This is the legacy of the Glorious Glosters.

Ron Brooks
Armistice Day: 11 November 2021

In Memory of my brother-in-law and
good friend Bryan Greenhill

EIN HERZ FÜR AUTOREN A HEART FOR AUTHORS À L'ÉCOUTE DES AUTEURS MIA KAPΔ
HARTA FÖR FÖRFATTARE UN CORAZÓN POR LOS AUTORES YAZARLARIMIZA GÖNÜL
CUORE PER AUTORI ET HJERTE FOR FORFATTERE EEN HART VOOR SCHRIJVERS TEM
ZÖINKÉRT SERCE DLA AUTORÓW EIN HERZ FÜR AUTOREN A HEART FOR AUTHOR
ZAÇÃO BCEЙ ДУШОЙ K АВТОРАМ ETT HJÄRTA FÖR FÖRFATTARE Á LA ESCUCHA DE
EURS MIA KAPΔIA ΓΙΑ ΣΥΓΓΡΑΦΕΙΣ UN CUORE PER AUTORI ET HJERTE FOR FORFA
YAZARLARIMIZA RZÖINKÉRT SERCE DLA AUTORÓW E
OR SCHRIVERS RAÇÃO BCEЙ ДУШОЙ K АВТОРАМ ETT

The author

Ron Brooks was born on 14 November 1938, less
than ten months before the outbreak of World
War Two, which then lasted six years. Their house
was close to Filton Airfield, Bristol Docks, and
Avonmouth Docks, all prime target zones for the
Nazis. His dad was conscripted in 1940 and sent
abroad for almost five years, immediately after
compassionate leave following the very difficult
birth of Ron's brother Peter. Peter was born on
Sunday 13 April 1941 during the horrific Easter
bombings. Ron has clear memories of their ceil-
ings coming down, windows being blown in and
nearby houses demolished.

Mum Emmy was left to bring up four children
alone, with little money, heat, food, or clothes.
The one thing the family always had in oodles
though, was lots of love. Ron went on to pass his
11-plus and go to Cotham Grammar School. He
spent 42 years in Local Government and is now
self-employed, and an Associate Consultant with
BSI.